Screaming on the Inside

Also by Jessica Grose

Soulmates

Sad Desk Salad

*Home Economics: How Couples
Manage Their Money*

*Love, Mom: Poignant, Goofy,
Brilliant Messages from Home*

Screaming on the Inside

The Unsustainability of American Motherhood

Jessica Grose

MARINER BOOKS

New York · Boston

HarperCollins books may be purchased for educational, business, or sales promotional use. For information, please email the Special Markets Department at SPsales@harpercollins.com.

FIRST EDITION

Library of Congress Cataloging-in-Publication Data

Names: Grose, Jessica, author.
Title: Screaming on the inside : the unsustainability of American
    motherhood / Jessica Grose.
Description: First edition. | New York, NY : Mariner Books, [2022] |
    Includes bibliographical references and index.
Identifiers: LCCN 2022021876 (print) | LCCN 2022021877 (ebook) | ISBN
    9780063078352 (hardcover) | ISBN 9780063078369 (trade paperback) | ISBN
    9780063078376 (ebook)
Subjects: LCSH: Motherhood—United States. | Mothers—United States. |
    Parental leave—United States.
Classification: LCC HQ759 .G8175 2022 (print) | LCC HQ759 (ebook) | DDC
    306.874/3—dc23/eng/20220520
LC record available at https://lccn.loc.gov/2022021876
LC ebook record available at https://lccn.loc.gov/2022021877

ISBN 978-0-06-307835-2

22 23 24 25 26 LSC 10 9 8 7 6 5 4 3 2 1

To my daughters

Contents

Introduction

I failed at ideal motherhood before I even had a child. I felt as if I had ruined it all by the time I was six weeks pregnant with my older daughter.

I thought I had done everything correctly. I was twenty-nine when I got pregnant because I had read the statistics about how much harder it is to conceive as you get into your thirties.

I was financially stable and happily married and college educated and debt-free.

I had begun a shiny new job in a leadership role, because Sheryl Sandberg said, "Don't leave before you leave," in a TED Talk,[1] which is to say, if you're ambitious, don't take your "foot off the gas pedal" in your career before you even have children. Despite priding myself on not being the type of chump seduced by TED Talk platitudes, especially those delivered by Facebook executives, I'm embarrassed to say I listened to this one.

I went off antidepressants to conceive because I felt I needed to be as "natural" as possible. I still don't know where I got this notion, except from the maternal expectations that had seeped into me through some kind of demented osmosis. The doctors around me didn't tell me I had to get off the medication, but they didn't stop me from going off it, either. None of them told me the relapse rate for pregnant women who discontinue their antidepressants may be as high as 68 percent.[2]

I found out I was pregnant on my second day of that shiny new job, and I had about a week of grace before it all fell apart. I started vomiting uncontrollably, at least five times a day. Some days I held nothing down at all. I had breakthrough bleeding at seven weeks. My depressive and anxious symptoms came roaring back shortly after I started throwing up, ultimately becoming so extreme that I could barely leave the house because I was afraid of both barfing on the subway *and* sarin gas attacks.

Though I had covered family policy as a journalist, it had never fully registered for me that you needed to work somewhere for a year to qualify for even unpaid parental leave through the Family and Medical Leave Act.[3] I felt deeply stupid when I realized this—of all people, I should have known better. In fairness to my former self, this information is deliberately confusing and hard to access. Even in the states that offer paid parental leave, so many parents are leaving support on the table because they don't even know that it is available to them.[4]

I had to tell my new boss I was pregnant very early on because I was so sick, and while he was sympathetic as a human, the systems surrounding us could not support what I was going through. When I realized that it would be a struggle to get short-term disability, and that my job might not ultimately be protected, I quit. I figured I probably would have been fired soon anyway because I was doing such an awful job. I assumed my career was finished.

To quit was an act of privilege. I had health insurance through my husband's job, and we had no debt and our own safety nets, not to mention parents who could support us if it came to that. But quitting was also an act of self-preservation. I did not think I would survive my pregnancy if I did not put my own health before my employment.

It was the right choice in retrospect, even if it took me years to feel halfway decent about making it.

My very early failure at doing motherhood "right" served as a moment of revelation. It became crystal clear to me that you could do everything that American society pressures you to do as an individual and as a mother, and if anything goes wrong, not only are you on your own, but you will also be either tacitly or explicitly blamed for your deviation. I have devoted much of my career since then to revealing how morally bankrupt so many of these ideals are.

In 2020, that moment of revelation hit nearly every mother in the United States. When the shit hit the fan during the COVID-19 pandemic, and all the rickety systems of care, school, and health collapsed in an instant, we all learned how alone we were. We were expected to teach our children, perform our jobs, and keep everyone in our orbit healthy, sometimes all in the same minute. We decided to have babies in the first place, so how dare we demand any help at all?

But while the parenting fiasco of COVID-19 was a crisis, it was also the culmination of more than two hundred years of unrealistic, elitist, and bigoted expectations, and the laws that flowed out of those expectations. What is so insidious about these ideals is that they shape-shift; they reflect whatever is in vogue—but at their core is always self-abnegation.

In the early days of colonial America, the ideal was a pious white Christian woman who spun cloth with her baby at her heels and helped keep her children on the straight and narrow path to salvation. Over the next few centuries, new requirements appeared: a focus on creating stalwart American citizens, and an education in scientific child-rearing techniques. God help you if you weren't keeping up on the latest expert trend.

In our current era, the perfect mother is a woman who seamlessly melds work, wellness, and home. She is often blond and thin. Her roots are never showing, and she installed that gleaming kitchen backsplash herself (watch her TikTok for DIY tips because the public projection of this perfect motherhood is part of the deal).

She single-handedly runs remote school and still finds time to meditate at 5:00 a.m. Her children are a glossy reflection of her efforts, never a spot on their clothing or a frown on their faces. Even as she is expending maximal effort at home, she still behaves like an "ideal worker" in her paid employment. The "ideal worker"—a term coined by legal and gender scholar Joan Williams—means working as if you have no family or health responsibilities.

Even if you consciously reject this litany of demands, they manage to worm their way into you.

What is obvious about these standards when you see them written out this way is not only how absurd they are, but also how individualistic and superficial these pressures can be. They have nothing to do with your private relationship with your own children, your values, or your needs.

The truth is that parenting cannot follow a recipe; there's no foolproof set of rules that will result in a perfectly adjusted child. Every parent has different values, and we will have different ideas about how to pass those values along to our children. While writing and researching this book, I spoke to around a hundred mothers, and my ultimate takeaway is that there are *so* many ways to raise healthy thriving children. What successful parenting has in common is not a particular set of rules, but close observation of the kind of unique humans our children are. As my opa, who was a family doctor in a small town, used to say, you cannot raise a daisy like an orchid.

The other thing that is noteworthy about the contemporary set of expectations is they don't engage with the broader community in any way, shape, or form. Rarely do babysitters, teachers, grandparents, aunties, uncles, or friends appear in heralded images of motherhood that are beamed into our phones. If the pandemic taught us anything, it should have taught us that we need to invest in our local, national, and international ties to raise the next generation.

No country in the entire world that is as wealthy as the United States gives as little to parents. Though there have been tremendous gains for mothers at work in the past fifty years, we still do not have federal paid parental leave or consistently subsidized childcare. Even parents in two-income families fear financial insecurity. The costs of childcare continue to soar—as one mother put it to me: "I pay pretty much my rent in day care."[5] And student loan bills haunt millions of parents, with no realistic hopes of forgiveness.

But I believe the pandemic has changed the game. In my decade-plus of covering work and family, more people of all political persuasions are talking about paid leave, the costs of childcare, and universal pre-K at the federal level than I have ever observed before.

It will be a long road toward systemic change, with many stutter steps along the way. But as of this writing, there is preliminary evidence that the expanded Child Tax Credit—direct payments into parents' bank accounts—has helped cut child poverty and hunger, and that parents have directed some of the funds into their children's education.[6] Though these credits expired at the end of 2021,[7] I hold out hope for some kind of more permanent change.

I believe this change is possible, despite so much political delay and dysfunction in our system, because I am regularly moved by stories of mothers who are working hard to improve their communities at home and channeling their energy into causes abroad, and I share some of those stories in these pages.

Because I know there's not a single way every person should raise their family, I am reluctant to give parenting advice. But if you have one takeaway from the history, sociology, science, and brand-new reporting in this book, it's that the ideals as they are created now serve almost no one. They may serve industry, but they do not serve us or our families.

Anytime you feel guilty about not meeting some sort of insane, unachievable demand, ask yourself: Does this help me improve my relationship with my children? And does this help my community? If the answer is neither, push back. Refuse to feel the guilt and failure that plague so many of us when we are just trying to raise our families under this broken system. Instead, use that energy to fuel something different: the possibility of a more humane and supportive future for our children.

I wish I could go back to myself a decade ago and tell her that she isn't a failure for being sick, for taking the medicine she needs, and for taking several months away from work to tend to her health and her newborn. If I could not be that voice for myself, maybe I can be that voice for others. You are making the best choices you can in a society that holds mothers to unachievable standards. In the next chapter, when you see the unjust genesis of many of our current mores, you might just realize you're doing a great job listening to your own values.

ONE

How Did We Get Here?

THE PERFECT MORAL VESSEL, STARTING
AT CONCEPTION

This chapter goes deep into the history of the American way of bearing and raising children. Although some of it may seem distant from the experiences of a modern mother, when you read the rest of the book, you will see how the roots of our current ideals were planted hundreds of years ago, and how they have split the ground we walk on today. If you are too exhausted from years of pandemic parenting to dive into the past, the stories of contemporary motherhood begin in chapter two. The history will still be here when you are less of an empty husk.

The idea that good mothers should be self-sacrificing prevailed for thousands of years. Early Christian, Jewish, and Muslim texts objectified women as "symbols of willing and selfless devotion."[1] As we entered the modern world, and medical technology progressed to create smaller families—and healthier babies and mothers—the image of "willing and selfless devotion" evolved.

No longer is the ideal mother a colonial woman waking up at

first light to churn butter while worrying about her children's immortal souls; now she's a perky modern mom organizing the vast dairy section of her spotless Sub-Zero refrigerator and worrying about property taxes. But one thing has remained consistent: despite the obvious and invisible work that mothers do to keep families and societies together, their contributions have either been insincerely praised, ignored, or actively demonized, depending on the time period, specific place, and a mother's social standing.

The expectation that a woman should be a perfect, moral vessel began at conception. In colonial times, the understanding of reproduction was that men provided all the material to make the baby—it was their seed and their seed alone that grew into a person. Even though a woman was considered useless in making a baby, "she was ascribed considerable power to damage the one a man generated in her," wrote Agnes R. Howard in *Showing: What Pregnancy Tells Us about Being Human*.

Early modern pregnancy manuals spent a great deal of time warning women that their thought crimes could alter their growing feti, and in general, women were thought to be more susceptible to the devil while they were pregnant and postpartum.[2]

The medical historian Mary Fissell calls this "the treachery of the maternal imagination."[3] For example, if a woman even thought about an adulterous lover during conception or pregnancy, her child would look like that man (and conversely, a woman could "inscribe her husband's looks on illegitimate offspring if she thought hard on it," Howard wrote). If a mother craved sea mussels, she risked having a baby with a sea mussel for a head. In 1726 England, a servant named Mary Toft convinced a lot of powerful people that she gave birth to a litter of bunnies after she was startled by a rabbit, though she was ultimately revealed to be a grifter.

If, while pregnant, a woman looked at a painting of John the Baptist wearing animal hides, she risked having a terrifyingly hairy baby. This story, repeated in colonial-era pregnancy guides, emphasized both how dim women are—that they thought an ascetic saint was a hairy animal just because he had a furry jacket—and how powerful their wayward minds could be. They could produce "a female monster from that distorted impression," wrote Fissell.

"RICH IS THE MAN WHOSE WIFE IS DEAD AND HORSE ALIVE"

Because there was so much work to be done in the home, and little industry in the outside world, fathers were quite involved in domestic life in early America, and the idea of the individual all-important mother didn't have quite the same weight as it does today.

In her book *American Work: Four Centuries of Black and White Labor*, Jacqueline Jones, a social historian, notes that women and children were considered "useless hands" in much of the early colonial experience in the Chesapeake region, which is modern-day Virginia and Maryland. "Since most early settlements more nearly resembled frontier outposts than traditional English villages, women possessed virtually no necessary skills that men themselves could not supply, and they might even prove to be a distinct liability if they could not help to defend the colony with a sword or a gun."[4]

"Respectable" white English women in the Southern colonies were supposed to help their countrymen re-create nuclear families and civilize them as a way to maintain state order. They tried to replicate the domestic division of work that existed in England, where women did the caretaking, spinning, sewing, and baking, while men chopped wood and managed the land.

But in the early days of settlement, there was a labor shortage, an extremely high mortality rate, very few women overall, and an "infinite supply of land," so men performed "masculine housewifery" and even some white women who were not indentured servants worked in the fields in the seventeenth century, Jones notes.[5]

Even with everyone partaking in similar labor early on, racialized divisions were emphasized, and as soon as there were enough workers to separate white women from enslaved women, those divisions were codified, and white women wives and servants stopped working in the fields. According to Jones:

> As the seventeenth century wore on, Virginia prevented black men from bearing arms (1640), condemned black children and women to field work, as tithables (1642), decreed that the offspring of slave-women were slaves (1662), and that the conversion to Christianity did not bring freedom (1667). The colony's official slave code was passed in 1705.

Up in New England, the gender ratio was more equal. People lived longer and had more surviving children, and the structure of families was more stable.[6] Mothers had a defined role in these Northern households—they were below their husbands, but above their children and indentured servants.[7]

In these Northern colonies, "women's productive work took place primarily within the confines of their own households," writes the historian Mary Beth Norton.[8] And the running of a preindustrial home was incredibly demanding. There was no real separation between productive work and parenting. "New England housewives worked dawn to dusk: they planted and maintained kitchen gardens, spent hours each day building and tending to fires to heat homes and cook, baked bread and other foods, made cider and beer, traded and bartered for sugar, wine, spices, and other goods produced beyond the farm, spun and carded wool, sewed and ironed clothing," writes historian Jodi Vandenberg-Daves.[9]

Other academics, including Laurel Thatcher Ulrich, described mothering as "extensive" rather than "intensive"—which is the type of helicopter, highly involved mothering we do today. Extensive mothering meant "the experience of motherhood was shaped largely by the permeable household structure of colonial America, in which neighbors, friends, and kin played significant caretaking roles, and by a general dependence on Divine Providence for interpreting maternal experience," as Nancy Schrom Dye and Daniel Blake Smith explain.[10] Fathers were often present, as their work was often done in and around the home, and so they were intimately involved in their children's days.

Unlike today, where most guidance is directed toward mothers, in colonial times written guidance for parents was addressed to both mothers and fathers. "Faith, virtue, wisdom, sobriety, industry, love and fidelity in marriage, and joint obligations to children typically enjoined on both sexes," in Puritan literature, according to historian Ruth H. Bloch.[11]

Men in the sixteenth and seventeenth centuries were tasked with choosing and hiring wet nurses if breastfeeding was not possible, according to Hugh Cunningham, a historian of childhood. "Fathers should watch over their children, thoughtfully interpreting 'every little action, word and gesture' so as to understand the nature and probable future destiny of their child."[12] Fathers were considered just as, if not more, important as mothers in raising a child because they were seen as ultimately responsible for a child's character.

"For many women, personal piety became a form of nurture," wrote Thatcher Ulrich, of colonial mothers in New England. They did not have the time or energy to pay attention to their big broods because they were busy working.

As a result, many of their young children died in horrific accidents, like falling into wells and fires. "With heavy responsibilities, little time, and few resources, they could at least admonish and pray." These Puritan women did not expect to find happiness in their children, or in this world at all; happiness was only available if you were saved in the afterlife. A mother could only hope that her offspring, marred by sin, made it to heaven.

Specific mothers were seen as so nonessential to the process of raising children that there was an old peasant French proverb that went something like, "Rich is the man whose wife is dead and horse alive." As Lawrence Stone, a historian of English history, explained, "If necessary, the wife could be replaced very cheaply, while the family economy depended on the health of the animal."[13] A wet nurse could be procured to nourish the children, a new wife found to warm a man's bed. But a great horse was irreplaceable.

"THE HUSBAND WAS THE FAMILY'S ECONOMIC MOTOR, AND THE WIFE ITS SENTIMENTAL CORE"

The individual mother began to matter as the US moved toward its Revolution. That identity—the insistence that "the home must be guided by a calm, devoted and self-abnegating wife and mother,"[14] as historian Nancy Cott puts it—began to coalesce in the eighteenth century and was fleshed out in the nineteenth century. Fathers were pushed out and discouraged from closer relationships over time.

In the colonial period, goods were produced largely within households. Though fathers were the supervisors of this family labor, according to the historian Stephanie Coontz, mothers were an integral part of the work.[15] When the production of goods shifted to factories and other spaces outside the home, women's domestic labor lessened, but households depended on earnings to purchase items previously made at home. Here, women began to fall into a trap: they were discouraged from sullying themselves with wage earning, which was associated with a lack of femininity and moral standing, but idleness was also considered a vice. Motherhood became their work. As Coontz lyrically put it, "The husband was the family's economic motor, and the wife its sentimental core."[16]

What this meant practically is that two separate spheres were created over time: the public sphere and the domestic sphere. This more distinct separation was a mixed bag for women. On one hand, they were held up by society and sentimentalized in a way they had not been before; mothers were no longer compared unfavorably to horses, is what I'm saying. But on the other hand, in encouraging women to remain in the domestic sphere, society prevented them from holding any social power under the false guise of protecting them. As Coontz explains:

> No longer was the exclusion of women from political and economic power explained in terms of male power or privilege, as had been frankly admitted in the past. Many men and women came to believe that wives should remain at home, not because men had the right to dominate them, but because home was a sanctuary in which women could be sheltered from the turmoil of economic and political life. Conversely, the domestic sphere became a place where husbands could escape the materialistic preoccupations of the workaday world of wages.[17]

As a result, childcare became the core of a woman's duty at home, and as women's magazines, sermons, and parental guidebooks began to tell women in the early nineteenth century, they should find happiness in their domestic duties, or there was something wrong with them, and they posed a threat to society.

Which is not to say the wealthiest among mothers of the eighteenth and early nineteenth century did many of the boring or difficult tasks—those were outsourced. Many children of the elite "did not spend much time in the loving arms of vigilant 'moral mothers,' but instead were under the care of immigrant or Black domestics," as Sharon Hays puts it in *The Cultural Contradictions of Motherhood*.[18]

And vaunted cultural sentimentality was reserved for white Protestant mothers. Enslaved Black mothers were denied even the barest human consideration, as Dorothy E. Roberts explains in her groundbreaking book *Killing the Black Body: Race, Reproduction, and the Meaning of Liberty*. These mothers were often separated from their children; and all their offspring, even the children who were the products of sexual assault by their enslavers, were considered property. "Black women in bondage were systematically denied the rights of motherhood. Slavery so disrupted their relationship with their children that it may be more accurate to say that as far as slaveowners were concerned, they 'were not mothers at all,'" Roberts writes.[19]

CREATING "VIRTUOUS CITIZENS OF THE REPUBLIC"

The changes in economic roles for women in the aftermath of the American Revolution dovetailed with the concept of "the republican mother," which is the idea that it's also a mother's job to create up-standing American citizens—or else the nascent country might fall apart. This was meant to paper over the inconsistencies of a citizen-led democracy that did not allow any non-white, non-male citizens to participate in it. As Linda Kerber, a legal historian, wrote in her landmark article about republican motherhood, "Direct political participation and influence require voting and office-holding. American intellectuals who sought to create a vehicle by which women might demonstrate their political competence shrank from that solution . . . to do so would have required a conceptual and political leap for which they were apparently not prepared."[20]

Although she could not vote or run for office, a republican mother had an important societal role: to raise sons and discipline husbands "to be virtuous citizens of the republic."[21] In the late eighteenth century, voting was mostly restricted (with a few notable exceptions[22]) to white male landowners over twenty-one. The Naturalization Bill of 1790 explicitly defined citizenship as only for "white immigrants," which in practice meant people from Western Europe.[23]

The imperative to rear new citizens gave wealthy white mothers a certain kind of soft power and differentiated them from mothers of other races, but at the same time, it also confined them away from the public sphere. Per Kerber, "The learned woman, who might very well wish to make choices as well as influence attitudes, was a visible threat to this arrangement."[24]

The writings of Mary Palmer Tyler, a New England wife and mother who lived from 1775 to 1866, illustrate the vaunted expectations put on post-Revolution women. Mary had eleven children over a period of sixteen years, and her husband, Royall, who was a member of Vermont's Supreme Court, was frequently away from home.

She learned how to take care of her first baby from her mother. But when her family moved away, Palmer Tyler began to rely on parenting books, which emphasized a mother's natural, biological relationship to her children. "As 'sweet pledges of connubial love,'" Palmer Tyler believed "children were the source of a woman's happiness," the independent scholar Marilyn S. Blackwell notes.[25]

Palmer Tyler wrote her own childcare manual in 1811, where she explicitly laid out her vision of the ideal mother: "To say nothing of our duty, as *citizens*, while forming the future guardians of our beloved country, it is undoubtedly our duty, as *mothers*, to bring up our sons in such a manner as shall render them most useful and happy," and to bring up daughters to raise the following generation of upright sons. "The future beauty, health, and happiness of the rising generation, and eventually, the welfare of the community at large" was all up to the new American mother.[26]

Another nineteenth-century parenting manual, Catharine Beecher's bestseller *A Treatise on Domestic Economy*, originally published in 1841, is an excellent example of the way motherhood was transformed into a specific kind of work during that era. Beecher, the sister of Harriet Beecher Stowe, was anti-suffrage because she believed that women's considerable energies needed to be funneled exclusively into the domestic sphere, and that working for wages or engaging in politics would be too distracting and morally compromising.

"A large majority of American women would regard the gift of the ballot, not as a privilege conferred, but as an act of oppression, forcing them to assume responsibilities belonging to man, for which they are not and can not be qualified; and, consequently, withdrawing attention and interest from the distinctive and more important duties of their sex," Beecher wrote.[27]

Beecher argued that mothers needed to be educated for their profession, and that domesticity should be elevated to a science just like politics—the entire moral virtue of the nation depended on it.[28] "The mother forms the character of the future man; the sister bends the fibres that are hereafter to be the forest tree; the wife sways the heart, whose energies may turn for good or for evil the destinies of a nation," Beecher wrote. "The proper education of a man decides the welfare of an individual; but educate a woman, and the interests of a whole family are secured."

"THE MOTHER FORMS THE CHARACTER OF THE FUTURE MAN"

The idea that parenting had defined goals meant that motherhood began to be something at which you could succeed or fail. No longer were children's fates in the hands of God alone; now they were in the hands of America's mothers.

The main work of wealthy Southern mothers in the nineteenth century was perpetuating their children's elite status through education and nurturing their individual identities and skills, according to the historian and novelist Katy Simpson Smith.[29] Shaping their children was one of the few forms of power, control, and meaning that elite women had at their disposal. It also became central to their own sense of identity.

These white women wanted to separate themselves and their children from the other women in their orbit: working-class women, enslaved women, and Native American women. Mothers in the South raised children "who embodied the intangible virtues of honor, civic duty, and gentility. Ensuring that their sons learned Latin, their daughters spoke French, and their toddlers stayed away from enslaved children, many elite mothers helped define an exclusionary class."[30]

Though there were some differences in different regions of this vast country, for the majority of American women, "I think that there was the expectation that mothers would devote themselves entirely to their children and sacrifice themselves for their children as well," said Anya Jabour, a professor of history at the University of Montana, whose research focuses on nineteenth-century women and families. "Once they became mothers, a lot of women shifted from looking for happiness in their marriage to looking for happiness in their motherhood. They previously had sought emotional satisfaction from their husbands, which was not necessarily forthcoming."[31] Their husbands might be away from home for weeks or months at a time, and they obviously couldn't text a cry for help if they were suffering in the moment.

Reading about these women and their desire for recognition and satisfaction from their children's achievements feels familiar.

You can hear echoes of their efforts in the modern arms race to catapult children into elite colleges. In its most extreme version it's the farce of the 2019 college bribery scandal, where wealthy parents paid a consultant to photoshop their middling students into water polo matches so that they might attend USC.[32]

And also similar to today, the pressure to raise perfect, healthy citizens and find deep meaning in that pursuit created guilt and anxiety. Even in the nineteenth-century South, breastfeeding was a flashpoint among elite white mothers. "Though wet nurses, including enslaved ones, were employed when elite women had difficulty nursing, the majority of southern women in the eighteenth and early nineteenth centuries breastfed their own children," according to Simpson Smith.[33] Breastfeeding earned women hosannas from their community, and their peers helped to enforce their cultural norms.

Some women loved to breastfeed their children and felt joy and warm intimacy in their nursing relationship. Other women experienced a great deal of pain and suffering. A young mother named Eliza Haywood wrote, "Fabius keeps me awake what few hours I have to sleep by getting up so often to Suck, for I am up every Night till Twelve or one O'clock at Night, preparing for the next day's Dinner; and then when I go to bed he disturbs me so often I can't Sleep, and the other Boys wake me by Day break."[34]

Eliza also experienced a painful abscess, without the benefit of modern medicine. "I had Excruciating pains in my Shoulders, Breast and Stomach," Eliza wrote to her mother. "The discharge of Matter was great with much Blood. It still runs a deal twice a day, Night and Morning."[35] Only Eliza's mother cared about these maladies; Eliza's husband was not especially sympathetic. He encouraged her to wean so that she might pay more attention to him, though that raised the risk of Eliza becoming pregnant again. Breastfeeding was also one of the few ways women could control their fertility at the time—although it's possible to conceive while still nursing, pregnancy is less likely.[36]

"I FEEL PROUD TO BE THE PIONEER TO LESS SUFFERING FOR POOR, WEAK WOMANKIND"

While mothers were being told that they had a great deal of power to transform their children, another societal current tried to convince them that they were physically and psychologically weak: Medical advances in the nineteenth century were often used to justify keeping mothers from having any real societal force, or control, over their own bodies.

Though pregnancy manuals existed before the 1800s, women in the colonial era tended to learn about childbirth from their own mothers, sisters, and community-based midwives, who could share the unpleasant realities of pregnancy firsthand without sugarcoating it. Prenatal care barely existed, women gave birth at home, and men were typically tossed out of the house while women were in labor.[37]

Scientists did not set eyes on female human eggs until 1827,[38] and it wasn't until the end of the nineteenth century that the equal role of egg and sperm in reproduction was fully acknowledged. Before the twentieth century, women did not know for sure they were pregnant until they were four or five months along and felt the baby move—early signs of pregnancy like vomiting and missed periods could also signal other issues, such as disease or malnourishment.

That started to change as the nineteenth century wore on because of a confluence of two main factors: doctors moving into childbirth to gain control of the care of pregnant women, and a culture that was desperately trying to keep white women at home, having as many children as possible.[39]

A major medical advance came in 1847, when James Young Simpson, a Scottish obstetrician, discovered that ether and chloroform could make childbirth a much less painful experience for women.[40] That year, the first American woman received ether during birth. Her name was Fanny Longfellow, and she freaking loved it.

"I never was better or got through a confinement so comfortably," she wrote in a letter to her sister-in-law. "I feel proud to be the pioneer to less suffering for poor, weak womankind. This is certainly the greatest blessing of this age, and I am glad to have lived at the time of its coming and in the country which gives it to the world."[41]

At the same time, medical schools were churning out more and more trained physicians. Obstetrics was a somewhat new and lucrative frontier for them—and they needed to drum up patients. That healthy dose of chloroform, which midwives could not provide, was attractive to middle- and upper-class women like Fanny Longfellow. Physicians also promised a safer birth, through use of medical instruments like forceps.

Though doctors were not always able to deliver on those promises—"It bursts your brain, and tears out your heart, and crushes your nerves to bits. It's just hell,"[42] said one nineteenth-century woman who used a doctor instead of a midwife—women still began to flock to hospitals. This pushed local midwives out of the traditionally female birth industry, and shifted knowledge about pregnancy and birth to distant, often male experts.

Many doctors genuinely wanted to improve birth outcomes and cause women less pain during childbirth. But not all of them had beneficent aims: some conservative doctors were also part of a societal movement to increase the birth rate among white Protestant women, and give women less control over their reproductive lives (which happened to dovetail nicely with their financial interests). The birth rate fell from around 7 children per family at the beginning of the nineteenth century to around 3.5 by the end of it.[43]

According to the historians Carroll Smith-Rosenberg and Charles Rosenberg, "The Victorian woman's ideal social characteristics—nurturance, intuitive morality, domesticity, passivity, and affection—were all assumed to have a deeply rooted biological basis." Doctors and biologists argued that white women were physically and mentally frailer and their entire nervous system was attached to their uterus.[44] They thought that women's natural destiny was to have children, and that spinsters would experience more illness than mothers did.

Pregnant women's fragile minds were of great concern to these scientists. They believed that if a pregnant woman did not live "healthfully" her babies would be deformed. According to Shannon Withycombe, an associate professor of history at the University of New Mexico who studies nineteenth-century women's health and reproduction, doctors cautioned that many, many behaviors and feelings could cause miscarriages. "It's not just riding on horses. It's things you might smell or see. You should not experience any extreme emotion: not extreme sadness or extreme joy. You should not go out dancing, or read exciting novels," she explained.[45]

This focus on the biological fragility of mothers happened at the same moment when women wanted to have fewer children so they could become more active in society. "Middle- and upper-class white women were leaving home more for shopping, for entertainment and activism," Withycombe said in an interview.[46] They were getting involved in the suffrage and temperance movements. This was not appealing to men in power, who did not want women in public spaces, and they began pushing the idea that a "good" mother was one who was blissfully and modestly at home gestating a baby, rather than out in the streets. And some traditionalist researchers started coming up with biological theories that explained why women were unfit for anything but motherhood. These theories conveniently separated and idealized white Christian women over new immigrants and former slaves.

"LADIES" . . . AND EVERYONE ELSE

If mothers were too mentally and biologically fragile to go shopping for a petticoat, that they should not work outside the home almost goes without saying. Even working-class women tended to stop paid labor after marriage—by the Civil War, half of women never worked for pay, and of the remaining half, two thirds stopped working after they wed, according to the historian Alice Kessler-Harris in *Out to Work: A History of Wage-Earning Women in the United States*.[47]

Though Kessler-Harris also notes that many working-class mothers of young children would find a way to work from home, and they did not necessarily get counted as "workers." "In the days when they were having babies and the babies were small, they might take in boarders, take in laundry or sewing at home, or plant a vegetable garden in order to stretch a husband's income," she said in an interview.[48]

As Kessler-Harris notes, because middle-class and wealthy women never worked outside the home for pay, "a widening gulf stretched between them and those in the poorest jobs. This distance left wage-earning women particularly vulnerable," and it made wealthier women mostly unsympathetic to the plight of their employed sisters.[49]

In short, there were "ladies," pious, submissive, good white Christian mothers who maintained a beautiful and clean house, and there were mothers who worked outside the home for pay, who were seen as either frivolous for choosing to work when they didn't absolutely have to, or immoral because they were abandoning their children. Many women who worked in factories or as domestic workers in the North were either recent immigrants or free Black women.[50]

Women working for pay, whether they were mothers or not, made some progress during the Civil War, when their paid labor was essential to the economy. They participated in labor organizing and argued that because so many potential and current husbands perished in the war, it was appropriate for women to earn money.[51]

After the Civil War, a greater number of women began fighting for property rights and other types of legal standing. But overall, the cultural perception was that men should be supporting women, and if women were earning money, the men were failures. "This both exacerbated [a woman's] sense of dependence, and helped isolate men in an endless search for upward mobility and financial success," Kessler-Harris argues.[52]

As the nineteenth century drew to a close, women were moving into the wage labor force outside the home in greater numbers, and they were moving into higher education as well. An 1899 book called *What Women Can Earn: Occupations of Women and Their Compensation*, crowed about the wide array of professions open to the fairer sex—"Nearly every trade and profession is open to her," from grave digging to bookbinding.[53]

Even though you could break ground as a lady gravedigger, the explicit and implicit implication of every chapter in the book is that you would leave the workplace when you got married.

The chapter on women photographers explains that women "are better than men in modern photography—printing and retouching confided to feminine fingers—only one trouble, they marry too soon." The authors continue, "Almost every young girl goes into photography as she does into another trade or business, as a stepping-stone to matrimony . . . Women when married rightly expect that they are to be no longer breadwinners, and rarely pursue their occupations with the earnestness and intensity that they would if the idea of marriage were not constantly before them."[54]

THE RISE OF "SCIENTIFIC MOTHERHOOD"

Even though it may have been stifling for many, the nineteenth-century's focus on children for upper-class white women was fairly straightforward, and it was culturally rewarded. Children were expected to stay physically and emotionally close to their birth families as adults,[55] and mothers were allowed to show a great deal of gushy sentimentality toward their children. Elizabeth Scott Neblett, a mother who lived in Mississippi and Texas in the mid-nineteenth century, described a mother's love as "the holiest passion in the human breast."[56]

As the twentieth century began, that kind of maternal passion was seen as suspect, and even psychologically damaging. Child and maternal mortality declined precipitously, millions of Americans moved into cities and away from closer-knit communities, and women were granted a slew of rights in the latter half of the twentieth century that would have seemed unimaginable to their counterparts a hundred years before. Although these advances were much needed, they had the perverse effect of narrowing the qualifications of the ideal mother to a ridiculous and contradictory collection of traits.

Just as with childbirth and the movement from female midwives to male physicians, scientific motherhood came into full bloom by the early twentieth century. Scientific motherhood is "the belief that women require expert scientific and medical advice to raise their children healthfully,"[57] according to Rima D. Apple, a historian of motherhood. She continues:

> As it developed in the nineteenth century, women were exhorted to seek out information for themselves. By the twentieth century, women increasingly were told that they continued to be responsible for the well-being of their families, but needed to follow the

directions of their physicians. Such instruction positioned mothers
as both responsible for their families and incapable of that responsibility.

The twentieth century saw a massive proliferation of child-
rearing manuals, beginning with a Swedish feminist named Ellen
Key in 1900.

Key wrote a book called *The Century of the Child*. The book was
an international success, translated into several different languages,
including English, in 1909. In other works, Key argued that motherhood should be treated like a profession, that feminists of her day
were too focused on getting equal economic footing with men in an
unfair, capitalist society, and that the first three years of a child's life
should be heavily subsidized by the state. These are all thoroughly
modern notions we're still fighting about today.[58]

The underpinnings of Key's work were retro, though, and more
than a little eugenic. She believed that motherhood was a woman's
natural state, which is why it should be subsidized. If you didn't want
to be a mother, there was something wrong with you. It was also
your fault if your children were either mentally or physically unwell
because you were too young or too old, you didn't love your husband
enough, or had too many children, or were impregnated by a man
of poor character, or because you or your partner were "invalids."

"I am simply insisting that every woman, who has not yet ceased
to desire motherhood, has duties as a girl, still more as a woman, to
the unborn generation from which she cannot free herself without
absolute selfishness," she wrote.[59]

A good mother of young children could not possibly work or
socialize outside the home, Key believed, because she should never
be thinking of anything but her baby. "The child should be in one's
thoughts when one is sitting at home or walking along the road,
when one is lying down or when one is standing up," Key argued.

"This devotion, much more than the hours immediately given to one's children, is the absorbing thing; the occupation which makes an earnest mother always go to any eternal activity with divided soul and dissipated energy."[60] Certainly, childcare of any sort was out of the question for this devoted mother.

This was the energy percolating at the beginning of the twentieth century, a period of rapid change for women and mothers. As Ellen Key's muddle of beliefs demonstrates, for every step toward a new, more flexible identity for moms, there was a countervailing force, pushing back, demanding a rigid and unreasonable lockstep.

MOTHERS AS "SOCIAL HOUSEKEEPERS," SCRUBBING THE NATION CLEAN

The American government entered the business of pregnancy guidance in the twentieth century. The move to counsel pregnant women did not come from genuine concern about their well-being; it came out of a larger drive for children's health, and the health of women was only important insofar as it created healthier babies.

Infant mortality was still a major issue at the turn of the twentieth century. Though statistics weren't reliable, in the year 1900, experts estimate that as many as one in four children may have died before they turned five.[61] Pediatrics was not a defined specialty until the late nineteenth century, and poor children started working alongside their parents as soon as they could, in factories, on farms, and inside cramped apartments, as young as five or six.[62]

Because the birth rate had fallen, and the Industrial Revolution had allowed middle- and upper-class women to pursue domesticity full time, experts and manuals pushed to make housekeeping and baby-making into a science, with the underlying notion that health and wellness was not just a mother's responsibility, it was also totally under her control.

This gave mothers power at home, but it also caused them quite a bit of anxiety and guilt, argued the historian Regina Markell Morantz-Sanchez. She quotes the social reformer Paulina Wright Davis as saying: "Women are answerable, in a very large degree, for the imbecilities of disease, mental and bodily, and for the premature deaths prevailing throughout society—for the weakness, wretchedness, and shortness of life."[63] No pressure, though!

Still, this moral imperative inspired some middle- and upper-class women in the twentieth century to try to improve the health of all children, not just their own. Because social work was so intimately connected to their domestic work and their role as mothers, it was one of the few ways women could participate in the public sphere in even a marginally acceptable manner.

This was the backdrop for the creation of the Children's Bureau in 1912, the first federal agency to be laser-focused on the health and well-being of minors. It would not have been formed without the agitation of female progressives, and its first chief, Julia Lathrop, decided that her top priority was addressing infant mortality.[64] As part of this effort, starting in 1913 and lasting until the 1980s, the Children's Bureau published a booklet called *Prenatal Care*.

Much of the advice in the early editions of *Prenatal Care* is practical and helpful, and some of the basics (duration of pregnancy; early signs) still holds today. In the 1913 edition, the authors dispel the notion of "maternal impressions"—apparently, much of their readership still believed that having a baby with an ol' mussel head was still a possibility if they ate too many mussels.

But *Prenatal Care* does not absolve women of responsibility if something goes wrong with their baby. The 1913 guide does not have a section specifically about mental health. And yet it tells women that morning sickness is made worse by worrying, and also that if their pregnancy has a bad outcome, it's probably because of the mother's "failure to order her own life in the way that will result in the highest degree of health and happiness for herself and, therefore, for the child."[65]

Poor mothers and their children, of course, continued to work for pay, as they had in the nineteenth century. But as the Progressive Era began, activists like Florence Kelley, who was an upper-class divorced mother of three, began to agitate for better working conditions for working-class women and children. As head of the National Consumers League, Kelley advocated for the end of child labor and shorter working hours for women.[66] She and other reformers believed that if you changed the law to shorten working hours for women, which was an easier sell legislatively because the public was more sensitive to poor, defenseless ladies, labor laws for men would follow.

This did not mean that Kelley approved of working mothers, in theory. Despite the fact that she obviously worked, and was basically a single mother after she left her abusive husband, like most people in the aughts, she did not believe mothers should work in industry. "In families where the mother works for wages, the children suffer, if they do not die outright," Kelley said.[67] Domesticity for thee but not for me.

Kelley was a driving force behind a consequential 1908 Supreme Court decision, Muller v. Oregon, which on its face upheld a law that kept women from working more than ten hours a day, but ultimately ended up legally defining women as the more vulnerable sex, potential future mothers in need of protection.[68]

According to the Supreme Court decision: "That a woman's physical structure and performance of maternal functions place her at a disadvantage in the struggle for subsistence is obvious . . . Differentiated by these matters from the other sex, *she is properly placed in a class by herself,* and legislation designed for her protection may be sustained"[69] (emphasis mine). In practice, there were many loopholes to this law, and Black mothers were predictably left out.

Though Kelley arguably infantilized working mothers more than she improved their lives, she did demonstrate a way in which some patrician women entered the public sphere in the years leading up to World War I: activism. Groups like the General Federation of Women's Clubs, the National Association of Colored Women, and the Woman's Christian Temperance Union (WCTU) tried to help those in poverty in their communities, and in the case of the WCTU, snuff out booze, which they thought was the root of all social problems. "They became what one historian has called 'social housekeepers,'—willing to get down on their knees to scrub the nation clean," according to Alice Kessler-Harris.[70]

"IMMEDIATELY ONE MAY PROTEST THAT THESE WOMEN HAVE NO RIGHT TO BE MOTHERS AND HOMEMAKERS"

Just after World War I, women gained the right to vote, and the war effort had opened new vistas of possibility for mothers at work. Between 1910 and 1920, the number of married women working nearly doubled, from less than 5 percent to 9 percent.[71] (It's unclear how many of those women had children, but almost all married women of the day eventually did.) The majority of those women were working-class mothers who had no choice but to work for pay.

A 1926 study of a hundred professional women, done for the Bureau of Vocational Information, an early twentieth-century organization devoted to finding employment for the alumnae of elite women's colleges, treats working moms as if they are a foreign species. "There is the additional discovery that for the most part, these women are domestic and home loving to the same extent as their sisters who do not combine professional and home activities," the author Virginia MacMakin Collier wrote.[72] See, they're *not* monsters!

Although these career mothers were far from being considered the ideal ("Immediately one may protest that these women have no right to be mothers and homemakers," MacMakin Collier posits), they were mostly content. In fact, if you updated the language a bit, their statements could be coming from white-collar mothers a hundred years later. These mothers had supportive spouses who were happy to do some of the childcare, and they were proud of helping to support their families.

Mrs. R was a prime example of these new career mothers. "Mrs. R's interests are intellectual. She becomes irritable with the children and they with her when they are constantly together because they are so very much alike. She finds the manual labor connected with the children very tiring. It completely fatigues her and makes her ill," MacMakin Collier writes.

Another woman reported that once she returned to a full-time job, she was much happier, and she said that her relationship with her children was much improved. "When I was a more dutiful mother in the traditional sense I was certainly a crosser one," this mother said.[73]

Despite working outside the home, most of these professional mothers felt as if they should be doing everything in the domestic sphere as well, and they didn't want to ask for help. "More than one woman spoke of her conscious effort not to call on her family or her husband's family to help take care of the children or, in any way, to take responsibility she feels belongs to her and her alone," according to MacMakin Collier. "It is usually a man's pride to be financially independent when he sets up a family. It would appear that women, too, feel that they should hold up their end of the partnership without aid."[74]

That might be because just at the moment some mothers began to enter the workplace by choice, their contributions at home were being "disappeared" from the public ledger, Ann Crittenden argues in her 2001 bestseller *The Price of Motherhood*.[75] "The assumption that the unpaid labor of child-rearing has nothing to do with the real economy was cast in stone as early as the 1920s. By that time the official decision had been made to include in measures of the United States output only transactions in which money changed hands."[76]

What this meant, practically, is that the unpaid work of caring for children and home would never be counted in any official tallies, and it would not be supported in any real or sustained way by the federal government. A bare-bones welfare act for single mothers, widows, and impoverished families, called Aid to Dependent Children (ADC), was passed in 1935 as part of the New Deal. It was jointly funded by the federal government and individual states, and it allowed states to decide who received ADC funding.

Southern states deliberately excluded Black mothers from receiving support. As Dorothy Roberts notes in *Killing the Black Body*, "ADC was created primarily for white mothers, who were not expected to work. Black mothers, who had always been in the paid labor force in far higher numbers than white mothers, were considered inappropriate clients of a system geared to unemployable women."[77]

When the Fair Labor Standards Act,[78] which established the right to a minimum wage, was passed in 1938, the law excluded domestic workers, who were mainly Black and mainly Southern women. "Lawmakers hesitated to invade the home, a private space that defied inspection," according to Nancy Woloch.[79]

The twin crises of the Depression and World War II pushed more and wealthier married women into the workforce, and there was no turning back from this culture shift. During World War II, it was seen as a woman's patriotic duty to enter the workforce, to support her country and her husband overseas, whether or not she was a mother.

The Defense Housing and Community Facilities and Services Act of 1940, which was colloquially known as the Lanham Act, funded public works including childcare in communities with defense industries, the economist Betsey Stevenson notes. Under the provisions of the Lanham Act:

> All families (regardless of income) were eligible for childcare for up to six days a week, including summers and holidays, and parents paid the equivalent of just $9 to $10 a day in today's dollars. In addition to being affordable, this care was also high-quality. Many centers had low student-teacher ratios, served meals and snacks, and taught children arts and educational enrichment activities.[80]

Although the outcomes for the five hundred thousand children in these centers were excellent, and the mothers loved them so much they protested their closure, federal funding was shut off in 1946 after the war ended.[81] Women were expected to go back to their domestic roles without complaint, and the ideal white Christian woman was supposed to be perfectly content with her role as mother and homemaker.

"MADAM, YOU ARE TO BLAME!"

The desire for real careers happened alongside scientific advances that meant pregnancy and early childhood were less dangerous, and that women could finally control their fertility. By the middle of the twentieth century, the development and implementation of antibiotics and vaccines made infant mortality plummet. The decline was particularly sharp from 1930 to 1949, when death rates before a child's first birthday dropped 52 percent.[82] Maternal mortality followed a similar trajectory—it dropped over 70 percent from 1939 to 1949.[83] Meanwhile average family size was on the decline in part because of the invention of reliable and widely available birth control, a trend that continues today.[84]

You might think that when there was less fear of death, and fewer children to take care of, mothers might be more relaxed, and the pressures and expectations of motherhood might become less suffocating. Sadly, you'd be wrong. As a Lysol ad from a 1936 issue of *Good Housekeeping* put it: "Madam, *you are to blame!* . . . She'd have given her right hand to keep her baby well . . . yet that very hand may have caused the illness."[85]

By the 1950s, Freudian psychoanalysis and his ideas about the ego and a mother's impact on a child's psychosexual development all but defined popular ideas about anxiety, depression, and other mental illnesses.[86] It wasn't a conspiracy, but in postwar America, a handful of psychiatrists looking to make a name for themselves beyond their specialties realized that pregnant women during the baby boom were "an easy target," Ziv Eisenberg, author of "Clear and Pregnant Danger: The Making of Prenatal Psychology in Mid-Twentieth-Century America," told me. Theorizing about the damaged maternal mind got these shrinks "publicity beyond their immediate niche."

By pushing the idea that women who did not happily resign from their wartime occupations to become the ideal 1950s housewife were "neurotic," they identified a vexing social problem (women not knowing their place) and offered themselves as the solution (talk therapy, mild sedation, and rest could cure the most neurotic would-be mom of her woes).

Among these doctors were the brothers Karl and William Menninger, both prominent psychiatrists. "Some women openly despise all women and despise their own femaleness," Karl Menninger wrote in a major medical journal in 1939, explaining why some women were infertile. If these self-hating women did manage to get pregnant, he argued, they had terrible morning sickness.[87] In 1943, he wrote an article blaming an "ambitious business woman" for her own death because she didn't want to be pregnant in the first place, and she left her job only reluctantly. William Menninger believed that food cravings *and* morning sickness were both evidence of neurosis.

Other shrinks at the time blamed women for their own miscarriages, because either they had bad marriages or they had castrating mothers and weak fathers.[88] What was pernicious about the theories of these psychiatrists was how deeply their ideas were embedded in obstetric practices—and many of them served on state eugenic boards, deciding what patients should be sterilized.

Eisenberg tells a deeply upsetting story of a woman who had a history of hyperemesis. She had a previous miscarriage, one healthy child, and a therapeutic abortion when she was admitted to an Air Force hospital in Tacoma, Washington, in 1953, again barfing her guts out. Doctors told her she was immature, hysterical, and had an unhealthy attachment to her father. Though they did ultimately support her in having another healthy baby, doctors "feared the patient's 'emotional difficulties' would resurface and sterilized her." Eisenberg could not find out whether or not she consented to the procedure.[89]

Just as with its influence on pregnancy, Freudian psychology was massively influential in shifting our notions of ideal motherhood. Despite the fact that a handful of prominent female psychiatrists in the mid-century period had more realistic ideas about good mothers, and that many mothers pushed back against bizarre ideals, the dominant psychiatric narrative created a primrose path.

While in the late-nineteenth and early twentieth centuries an abundance of maternal affection was applauded, the cultural tide began to demonize overly loving mothers. By the postwar period, a mother had to worry about being both too affectionate *and* too cold. She was cautioned that the way she raised her child in his early years could destroy his psyche for a lifetime. Mothers "were expected to find a theoretical yet very subjective 'sweet spot' that doesn't really exist," Eisenberg said.

Nearly a million soldiers mentally unraveled during World War II, and why they did so became a matter of "great national concern," wrote Anne Harrington, a historian of science at Harvard.[90] A former president of the American Psychiatric Association and the surgeon general of the army and navy, Dr. Edward Strecker, blamed smothering mothers for what today we'd probably diagnose as post-traumatic stress disorder. These moms were "high-octane versions of the overprotective mother, all narcissistically invested in keeping their sons emotionally dependent on them, for their own gratification," Harrington notes.[91]

It wasn't just PTSD that mothers were blamed for in the 1940s and 1950s. If your child had autism or schizophrenia, that was your fault, too. Bruno Bettelheim, a child psychologist who fabricated his degrees, spread the notion that cold, emotionless mothers were primarily responsible for autism in their children.[92]

These so-called "refrigerator mothers" were also to blame for schizophrenic offspring. That notion came from small studies of schizophrenic patients, which found that their mothers tended to either reject or coddle their offspring.[93] Mothers of schizophrenic children were described in the psychiatric literature of the 1940s as "aggressive, over-anxious, over-solicitous and exhibited a marked ambivalence to these children."

Mothers internalized these messages. Rosalind C. Oppenheim, the mother of a son with nonverbal autism, was in the hospital recovering from a miscarriage around the time her child began to change. "Perhaps it was this enforced separation from me that triggered the change in Ethan that followed—we will never know," Oppenheim wrote in the *Saturday Evening Post* in 1961.[94]

The science writer Edward Dolnick summed up the mid-century

attitude toward mothers in the psychoanalytic community succinctly: "Like unwary tourists caught in a gang fight, these unfortunate parents happened to be in the wrong place at the wrong time. For mothers especially, to live in America in the 1940s, 1950s and 1960s was to stand convicted."[95]

At the same time, as Rima D. Apple persuasively argues in her book *Perfect Motherhood*, the pressures of parenting shifted even further toward the individual mother and the individual household. Popular TV shows of the 1950s, like *The Donna Reed Show*, *Father Knows Best,* and *Ozzie and Harriet*, depicted the ideal as a two-parent middle-class household with a father who worked and a mother who stayed home to raise the kids. A far cry from the "extensive" household of the colonial era, where extended family helped raise children and household boundaries were muddy.

This burnished image of the at-home married mom was venerated at a time when the number of women working and the number of single-parent households were beginning a steep ascent. The number of women with children under six in the workforce skyrocketed over the second half of the twentieth century. There is no good data on labor force participation of mothers with children under six from the first part of the century, but during the second half, "their labor force participation rate increased more than fivefold, from 12 percent in 1950 to 64 percent in 1998."[96]

"This disjuncture between popular image and lived experiences provided fuel for the mother-blaming of the postwar era, when social critics denounced women who stepped out of their traditional role for creating many of the problems of the day," including juvenile delinquency, divorce, and even death, Apple notes.[97]

The image of the 1950s ideal is still with us in commercials for household goods. She is ever-smiling, wearing an apron, and never has a harsh word for her beloved children as they streak across her just-washed kitchen. If she ever has a problem, she will figure out how to solve it, either with the help of approved experts, or by buying something—maybe from Lysol?

TRIUMPHS AND SETBACKS

But this expected domesticity contrasted with the growing number of mothers from all backgrounds in the workplace, and they began to agitate for equal treatment under the law. According to Alice Kessler-Harris, experts were stunned by the rapid entrance of mothers into the workforce: "It was too much to expect that women would continue to look on jobs as temporary. Even women who entered the work force for their families soon began to seek jobs in which they could use their skills to achieve appropriate rewards."[98]

Despite the pristine images of all-encompassing, self-abnegating motherhood that dominated mid-century pop culture, there were many real-life mothers who were miserable living that Donna Reed life. "By 1960, almost every major news journal was using the word *trapped* to describe the feelings of the American housewife," wrote the historian Stephanie Coontz. "When *Redbook*'s editors asked readers to provide them with examples of 'Why Young Mothers Feel Trapped,' they received 24,000 replies."[99]

"I became a mother in the family-centered, consumer-oriented, Freudian-American world of the 1950s," wrote the poet and essayist Adrienne Rich, in her 1976 work, *Of Woman Born: Motherhood as Experience and Institution*.

"My husband spoke eagerly of the children we would have; my parents-in-law awaited the birth of their grandchild. I had no idea what *I* wanted, what *I* could or could not choose. I only knew that to have a child was to assume adult womanhood to the full, to prove myself, to be 'like other women,'" Rich said of her identity struggles.[100] Rich was one of several prominent feminists, including Betty

Friedan and bell hooks, who would push back against the 1950s ideals in the 1960s, 1970s, and 1980s.

The Feminine Mystique, Friedan's bestselling book, created a tidal wave in this sea of discontent. Her 1963 publication gave a name to that dissatisfied, "trapped" feeling: the problem with no name. Coontz appraises the impact of *The Feminine Mystique* in her book *A Strange Stirring: The Feminine Mystique and American Women at the Dawn of the 1960s*, and finds that although Friedan left swaths of women out of her view—Black women who had been organizing for civil rights, and working-class women who always had jobs—she also galvanized a generation of women, born before the baby boom, to take stock of their lives and ask for more.

Coontz catalogs all the rights that women did not have until the 1970s and 1980s. In the 1960s, "many states still had 'head and master' laws, affirming that the wife was subject to her husband. And the expectation that husbands had the right to control what their wives did or even read was widespread." Only four states allowed married women to have their own legal residence, and it was almost impossible for a wife to rent or buy a home by herself. In many places, women were forced to take their husband's name upon marriage, and in five states, Coontz notes, women had to "receive court approval before opening a business in their own name."[101]

In 1966, Friedan; Dr. Pauli Murray, a Black lawyer, scholar, and civil rights activist; and several other women founded the National Organization for Women (NOW), which was dedicated to fighting for legal, workplace, and overall gender equality.[102] Throughout the late 1960s and early 1970s, women took to the streets, marching for legal recognition and against gender-based violence.

The federal government began to pass laws that supported fairer treatment of women at work. The Equal Pay Act, passed in 1963, established the principle of equal pay for equal work.[103] In 1964 came the Civil Rights Act, which technically forbade workplace discrimination on the basis of sex, though pregnancy remained a glaring exception.[104]

In the 1960s and into the early 1970s, it was still perfectly legal to fire a woman because she was pregnant, and many businesses required pregnant women to resign as part of their contract. Kessler-Harris told me that when she was a schoolteacher in Baltimore, "I signed a document that said if I got pregnant I would let them know within four months of my pregnancy, and I would quit my job when I began to show. This was perfectly normal in those days."[105]

It was still considered obscene by some for visibly pregnant women to be in public-facing work.[106] "Women faced a double bind because pregnancy forced them out of jobs, and at the same time made them ineligible for unemployment compensation," according to legal scholar Courtni E. Molnar.

Meanwhile, as part of the civil rights movement, Black activists fought to be included in welfare payments from ACD, renamed by this time Aid to Families with Dependent Children. But as Dorothy Roberts points out, "The activists had won a Pyrrhic victory . . . As AFDC became increasingly associated with Black mothers already stereotyped as lazy, irresponsible and overly fertile, it became increasingly burdened with behavior modification rules, work requirements, and reduced effective benefit levels."[107]

Though NOW gets most of the credit in the historical record, many other feminist organizations founded by and for the advancement of women of color were created in that second-wave period. As the feminist scholar Becky Thompson notes, Chicanas founded Hijas de Cuauhtémoc in 1971, Asian American women founded Asian Sisters that same year, Native American women founded Women of All Red Nations (WARN) in 1974, and Black women founded the National Black Feminist Organization (NBFO).[108]

The author and activist bell hooks pointed out in her book chapter "Revolutionary Parenting," published originally in 1984, the white and middle-class backgrounds of many early feminist organizers blinded them to the issues of Black mothers. "Had black women voiced their views on motherhood, it would not have been named a serious obstacle to our freedom as women," hooks wrote. "Racism, availability of jobs, lack of skills or education and a number of other issues would have been at the top of the list—but not motherhood. Black women would not have said motherhood prevented us from entering the world of paid work because we have always worked."[109]

Around the same time, many mothers were pushing back against the paternalistic excesses of the medical profession, especially around birth. Wendy Kline, a historian of medicine, calls these women "health feminists" in her analysis of three influential books about home birth written by midwives Ina May Gaskin, Raven Lang, and Rahima Baldwin. These women argued that by diminishing the work of midwives and moving birth into hospital settings, mothers "had been subjected to male medical authority; women could not achieve full equality without the right to reclaim their bodies."[110]

All of this organizing and activism opened the door for a wave of more nuanced and honest writing about early motherhood and identity formation from Adrienne Rich, Alice Walker, and Anne Lamott in the 1970s and 1980s, up to Sandra Tsing Loh, Dani McClain, Nefertiti Austin, and Angela Garbes much more recently.

In 1978, the Pregnancy Discrimination Act amended the Civil Rights Act to prohibit sex discrimination on the basis of pregnancy.[111] (Though to this day, pregnancy discrimination remains incredibly difficult to prove without medical documentation.[112]) These legal protections helped the rising tide of women in all sorts of paid work.

Though it's important to note that parents still had no federally mandated paid family leave, and childcare costs were just beginning their unabated rise.

The United States came close to establishing a federally funded childcare network in 1971, but President Nixon vetoed it, with a rebuke the *New York Times* described at the time as "stinging." He objected to the cost of the plan, but he also argued that government-supported childcare undermined the American family. "We cannot and will not ignore the challenge to do more for America's children in their all-important early years," Nixon said. "But our response to this challenge must be a measured, evolutionary, painstakingly considered one, consciously designed to cement the family in its rightful position as the keystone of our civilization."[113]

THE NEW FEMININE MYSTIQUE: SUPERMOM

In the aftermath of that bill's failure, federal childcare was a non-starter, but that didn't stop moms from taking paying jobs at all levels. As professional mothers flooded the workplace in the 1970s, 1980s, and 1990s, despite a basic safety net, the "supermom"—a star at work and at home—became the unrealistic ideal splashed on the cover of magazines.

"If you are a good mother, you must be an intensive one," argues Sharon Hays in *The Cultural Contradictions of Motherhood.* "Intensive" motherhood remains the dominant middle-class mode of child-rearing in the United States today—the organic fruit buying, code-class enrolling, travel soccer boosting, so-called "helicopter" or "snowplow" mom. Hays explains the very narrow options for the ideal mother:

> The only "choice" involved is whether you *add* the role of paid working woman. The options then, are as follows. On the one side there is the portrait of the "traditional mother" who stays home and dedicates her energy to the happiness of her family. This mother cheerfully studies the latest issue of *Family Circle*, places flowers in every room, and has dinner waiting when her husband comes home. This mother, when she's not

cleaning, cooking, sewing, shopping, doing the laundry, or comforting her mate, is focused on attending to the children and ensuring their proper development.

On the other side is the image of the successful "supermom." Effortlessly juggling home and work, this mother can push a stroller with one hand and carry a briefcase in the other. She is always properly coiffed, her nylons have no runs . . . Her children are immaculate and well-mannered but not passive, with a strong spirit and high self-esteem.[114]

Though Hays wrote these words in the mid-1990s, we have not moved past these ideals (except maybe the part about wearing "nylons" to work). In the past two decades we've simply added more expectations to the pile.

In the early 2000s, when Susan Douglas and Meredith Michaels wrote *The Mommy Myth*, they showed that the flawless egalitarian marriage with a loving spouse was a new wrinkle to the madness.

They described the supermom fantasy as a day when you get home from work, "joyfully empty the shopping bags and transform the process of putting the groceries away into a fun game your kids love to play . . . When your husband arrives, he is so overcome with admiration for how well you do it all that he looks lovingly into your eyes, kisses you, and presents you with a diamond anniversary bracelet. He then announces he has gone on flex time for the next two years so that he can split childcare duties with you fifty-fifty."[115]

By the 2010s, the burden of "self-care," which also includes a commitment to staying hot forever, was thrown on top of the expectations heap. "'Take care of yourself' = 'Take care of your looks,'" as the sociologist Debra Langan puts it.[116] You can never look haggard, like the pressures and time constraints of super motherhood are actually affecting you on any real level. You need to do it all and be it all without the forehead wrinkles that betray your efforts. In the past decade, we have also had the pressure to publicly perform our "good" mothering and #selfcare on social media, a topic that merits its own chapter later in this book.

The absurdity of the "supermom" has been obvious to many women for even longer. In a *Saturday Night Live* sketch by the late Anne Beatts that ran in 1975, a pulled-together mom enters the frame and starts unloading groceries.

ANNOUNCER: Meet Ellen Sherman, Cleveland housewife and mother.

HOUSEWIFE: Hi! I'm a nuclear physicist and commissioner of consumer affairs. In my spare time I do needlepoint, read, sculpt, take riding lessons and brush up on my knowledge of current events. Thursday is my day at the daycare center, and then there's my work with the deaf. But I still have time left over to do all my own baking and practice my backhand even though I'm on call twenty-four hours a day as a legal aide.

ANNOUNCER: How does Ellen Sherman do it all? She's smart. She takes Speed![117]

If it's been obvious for forty years that you need to be on stimulants and never sleep to accomplish all the things expected of a modern American mother, why do so many of us still buy into that myth, however subconsciously? And why aren't we pressuring society—and our communities—to help support parents in ways beyond empty platitudes? As Ann Crittenden put it in *The Price of Motherhood*, "All of the lip service to motherhood still floats in the air, as insubstantial as clouds of angel dust."[118]

Now that we've completed that occasionally hilarious (bunny grifts) and often infuriating (pretty much everything else) journey through the history of American motherhood, over the next several chapters we're going to see how that backstory shapes our experiences today.

It is present in the ideals and expectations we begin to feel the second we conceive or start the adoption process. It hovers over our beds as we toss and turn at night, trying to mentally fit together the puzzle of our schedules in a society that gives us little support when a snowstorm or COVID-19 outbreak closes school, a child barfs unexpectedly, or a last-minute work opportunity pops up after five. It lives in our phones, taunting us with physical perfection as we contemplate our eye bags (though maybe that's just me).

My own feelings of inadequacy began very shortly after I conceived. I was so sick, so soon, I could not even attempt to live up to the beautiful, competent, luminous expectations that lived in my head. In fact, my head was the last place I wanted to be.

TWO

Pregnancy

"YOU'RE A TRAILBLAZER!"

The tenth week of my first pregnancy felt like a single, unending day. I never slept.

Let's say it began at night. I crawled into bed. I knew that I desperately needed to sleep because I had to go to work the next morning with a functional brain. But I also knew that there was no way I would sleep. I had to get up at least once an hour to vomit up the three strands of pasta I had been able to choke down at dinner.

My body would not rest. Every single part of me felt coiled tight, a spring with enough energy to hurtle me into the ocean. I knew that I was failing at my new job because I could not concentrate because I could not stop throwing up. And the fewer nutrients my body got, the more my mind seemed to disintegrate.

No matter how hard I tried, I felt I could not properly nourish my body or my child, and I could not feel the joy that I thought a normal mother-to-be should feel. I did not want to go back on antidepressants. Though I was aware from talking to my doctors and to my mother, who is a psychiatrist, that the risks to the fetus from

SSRIs were modest, if my child had any issues, I knew I would blame myself for selfishly choosing relief over my baby's health.

At the same time, I knew that untreated maternal anxiety and depression *also* has modest risks for babies—ones very similar to the risks of medication—but somehow passivity felt less destructive than the active choice to take pills.

Over the preceding four weeks, as my depression and anxiety ramped up with each passing day, I had tried every non-medication remedy my psychologist recommended to ease my mind: weekly talk therapy, acupuncture, and breathing exercises that always ended in near-hyperventilation.

In week eight I tried to get a massage, and got so agitated halfway through that I started having a panic attack. I mumbled an apology to the soft-voiced masseuse, threw on my clothes, and bolted out the door sobbing, muffled whale sounds receding as I ran.

That night as I attempted sleep, I listened to a guided meditation on my headphones. This was in 2012, years before meditation apps littered the Apple store, promising deep, drug-free relaxation for the low, low price of $6 a month. I found the recording on a local university's mental health counseling website. It was in a section called "The Calming Corner," and a woman's gentle alto tried to lead me through a mental mountain walk, encouraging me to think about a rushing brook, and the crisp air around me.

But I could only think about the fetid air in my city bedroom and my agitated, sweaty body. I threw off the headphones and went to the bathroom to rest my head on the toilet, waiting for the inevitable. After it happened, I would pull myself up to the sink, wash my face and rinse my mouth with water; toothpaste made me gag.

I kept darting to the bathroom, my bed, and the kitchen. I thought that maybe drinking water or eating a few crackers would help settle my stomach, would stop my roiling mind. Nothing helped.

I spent part of the evening facedown on the cool tile of our kitchen, somehow convinced that I could finally fall asleep there.

Eventually I could see the sun peeking through slivers of window not covered by our blackout shades. My husband was still asleep. I pulled my laptop onto a pillow and tried to start my workday early. As the second-in-command of a popular culture website, part of my brief was to be on top of the news. So I sat in bed, scrolling through my RSS feed and Twitter, trying to find something, anything that was useful for the team. Instead my vision blurred with tears and my mind raced.

When my husband woke up, he rolled over and asked me how I was feeling. I hated when he asked me that question because the answer was always the same: miserable. And my response always upset *him*, which made me feel even worse.

My mother begged him to stop asking me how I felt because it always set up this circular call-and-response of despair. But he couldn't help himself—he felt scared and helpless, too.

It would take me hours after he left for work to shower, to get dressed, to get out the door and onto the subway. I was afraid of throwing up in public. But a larger terror loomed. What if there was a Sarin gas attack, like the one that death cult perpetrated in Tokyo in the 1990s? What if I fainted and fell onto the tracks? I pictured myself clinging to the filthy pillars at Chambers Street, thinking that if I held on to something welded into the ground, it would keep me from spinning out into the ether.

I had already told my boss I was pregnant. I hadn't wanted to tell him so soon, but I didn't feel like I had much choice. I thought the admission would make my life more tolerable—at least he would know why I was acting so strangely. But instead, his knowing only compounded my humiliation because it made every future interaction painfully awkward.

He was a kind man, and he did his best, but he had no idea how to deal with the situation. And the rest of the institution was not equipped to handle me in any sensitive way.

That endless day I went to HR to try to find out if there was any kind of short-term break I could take and still keep my job, and what my options would eventually be for maternity leave. I remember a perky woman I had never met before who had perfect beachy waves telling me the following things:

> You get six weeks of maternity leave for a vaginal birth and eight weeks for a C-section. Since you'll have been here less than a year, you're not eligible for that twelve weeks of unpaid leave from the Family and Medical Leave Act.
>
> You might be able to take some short-term disability during your pregnancy, but I have to look into it.
>
> You're the first person on the online side to take maternity leave! You're a trailblazer!

When she said the last part, I knew I was really screwed.

"YOU ARE OUT OF YOUR FUCKING MIND"

I recall the rest of the week only in flashes. Time became jagged, fragmented, and strange.

I remember trying to work on a story about Suzanne Somers. Long ago she made a career shift from ditzy blond actress to health and wellness guru, hawking nutritional and hormonal supplements and claiming to have discovered the true fountain of youth. My article was supposed to explain this transition, and it was pegged to the release of her twenty-second book.

Between trips to the bathroom, I did a deep dive into YouTube videos of ThighMaster infomercials. As I coughed up bile, I could still hear Somers's voice promising me that I could "squeeze, squeeze" my way "to shapely hips and thighs!"

I remember it didn't stop raining that week, but that may be a projection. I picture myself sitting up in bed, still clad in pajamas, staring out at a rain-soaked sidewalk, willing myself to get up, get dressed, and go to work. I can't remember how many days I actually made it out of the apartment.

I do have a vivid memory of calling in to one weekly meeting from home. Another editor was asking me when my Somers piece would be ready, and I snapped, "I don't know. As soon as I stop throwing up every ten minutes."

I could hear the stunned silence on the other end. I thought I was being a little sharp and funny, but it came off as unhinged.

I remember taking a cab to my psychologist's office one evening because I was still scared of the subway. I have absolutely no recollection of what was said in that session, except that I sobbed the entire time. I could not stop sobbing as I got into a cab to go back home. I called my friend Hanna from the car.

Hanna was my boss at the job I had left to take on this new role. She was more than that, though. She was a mentor, and also a friend. She had three kids and a soaring career and seemed to have figured out how to make it all work. From my perspective she plowed through barriers without apology; when she couldn't find a fridge at the office, she put her pumped breastmilk out on a window ledge in the January cold.

Some small part of me still wanted to believe that what was happening for me was within the realm of "normal." That I would not have to go back on antidepressants. Surely this sort of thing happened to lots of pregnant women? They just didn't talk about it.

As I cried over the phone to Hanna, trying to explain what was going on, she went silent for a minute. And then she said, not unkindly, "You are out of your fucking mind."

I still tried to get through the rest of the workweek because I felt I didn't have a choice. I had been assigned to go to a movie screening on Friday night, ahead of an interview with an actress who starred in it. I somehow clawed myself out of bed, put on clothes, and my husband escorted me to the theater, like an orderly propping up an elderly patient at a nursing home.

The movie was meant to be a comedy—a political satire about a dictator, though I could find no humor in the parts that I saw. I missed much of it anyway, sprinting to the bathroom constantly. Eventually I could no longer will myself to go back into the theater. I sat quietly sobbing on a bench outside the screening, which is where my husband found me.

We got into a cab, and my husband said something along the lines of: "You can't go on like this." I called the emergency line of my medicating psychiatrist and told him I absolutely needed to go back on medication.

He called me back immediately. He had already been talking to my psychologist and knew that I was struggling. Hearing my hysteria, he put through the prescription.

Since this wasn't my first antidepressant rodeo, I knew that once I started taking my meds, it would take a few weeks for them to kick in. But just knowing that I had taken a concrete step toward mental relief helped. For the past month I had felt like I was trapped in my misery, like I was covered by a scrim of unhappiness I couldn't take off. The hope of medication was a light coming through the fabric.

My new boss called me in the days after that. He told me that my behavior in that meeting—when I snapped about Suzanne Somers—

was unacceptable, and that I really did need to take some kind of leave.

He wasn't wrong. I told him I needed to think about what I wanted to do.

I had started taking my Prozac by then. But I still felt awful both mentally and physically, and I had no idea when I would start to feel better. It was suddenly very clear to me that I should quit.

I did not have it in me to worry about coming back to a job where I had humiliated myself, where no one respected me because I had not earned their respect. They only knew me as a vomiting wraith. But more than that: I did not want to go back to a full-time office job six weeks postpartum if I could help it. Even if I did by some miracle stop throwing up and crying, I didn't feel like it would be a good place for me as a mother. As the HR lady pointed out, I would have been the only one on the online side.

We were already on my husband's health insurance and could get by for a while on his salary alone. Though I was fairly convinced that quitting a job after two months would destroy the career I had spent a decade building, I did not see another option that I could live through. So I gave notice, and spent the entire month of June 2012 in bed.

Ten years later, I find this episode of my life painful to revisit. I still feel like I failed at some essential test of motherhood, before I even had a baby to care for. I *should* have been happier, or at the very least, I should not have lost my shit so thoroughly. I should have been stroking my growing belly and prancing through meadows in airy caftans, instead of barfing my life away in ratty T-shirts.

Intellectually, I know that pregnancy is manifestly uncomfortable and unfun for millions of women, and sometimes it's downright frightening, and even life-threatening. Somewhere between 7 and 20 percent of women experience perinatal anxiety and depression.[1]

Hyperemesis, which is morning sickness, like I had—so extreme that you lose 5 percent of your body weight or more—affects up to 3 percent of women, and is the most common reason for hospitalization in the first trimester.[2] Between 2 and 10 percent of women develop gestational diabetes.[3]

Every year, about seven hundred American women die from pregnancy complications.[4] Black women are three times more likely to die than white women; Native women are over two times more likely to die than white women; and Black babies are twice as likely to die in their first year as white babies.[5] Women hold all these painful truths and life-altering maladies in their bodies for nine months, brushing up against, and sometimes overtaking, the happiness they may also feel about having babies.

Though there have been many columns, books, and a million memes devoted to telling women that having difficulties during pregnancy is normal, those psychiatrists of the mid-twentieth century, who blamed women for their "neurosis" and morning sickness, did irrevocable damage.

The idea that there is something wrong with you if you're not happy and healthy while with child is so deeply embedded in our culture that these ideas are still expressed on TV and in film. On the show *Fleabag*, when the titular heroine's jerk brother-in-law thinks she's had a miscarriage, he says, "It's like a goldfish out the bowl sort of thing. If it didn't want to be in there. It didn't want to be in there. Something wasn't right. . . . WHAT? It's the kid's choice if it wants to jump ship, right?" (Fleabag punches him directly in the face after these words fall out of his mouth, as she should.)

At least I was lucky enough to have a supportive family that did not blame me for being sick, and didn't blame me for a miscarriage I had when my older daughter was two. I was also lucky to have a financial safety net that could cushion my job loss. Most women in America are not so amply blessed.

"I'D BE A GODDESS FLOATING ON A CLOUD"

Even after spending months researching this chapter, I was shocked at the pervasiveness and uniformity of women's visions of the ideal pregnancy. I spoke to women from all different backgrounds, many of whom had parents who were not American, and their notion of what their pregnancies should have been like were pretty much the same. "I had this perception I would feel ecstatic and joyous and I'd be a goddess floating on a cloud," said a woman I'll call Sadie, who identifies as Latina and Jewish and was pregnant with her second child when we spoke.

Like Sadie, all the women I spoke to envisioned a time of perfect happiness and Instagrammable beauty, where they would feel fulfilled and purposeful in ways they never had before. As Mohini Lal, who was born in North India and immigrated to the United States when she was three, put it, people expected her to "sparkle" when she was pregnant. "I did not sparkle. I did not feel sparkly, I did not look sparkly," she said.

I empathize with this statement—I had terrible acne during my first pregnancy and my hair thinned because I was throwing up all my nutrients. So, in addition to feeling awful, I looked like a mess. I remember sobbing on the way home from a dermatologist's office, because he told me there was nothing I could safely take during pregnancy to fix the way I looked. My own vanity embarrassed me as much as my livid complexion.

Most women I spoke to felt like they were failing on every possible level, inside and out. They described falling short of what their families, workplaces, and our culture wanted from them when they were publicly performing pregnancy. They also talked about how unwell they were, both physically and mentally, and how those feelings were compounded by guilt—they felt bad about feeling bad.

Candace Jackson had a hard time conceiving. When she ultimately got pregnant with her first child through IVF, she had already built pregnancy up as a "really idealized thing in my mind," she said. She always wanted to be a mom, and she fought so hard to get there. Her mother and sister both had easy pregnancies, and she thought it was something hereditary—she'd have an easy time, too. So she was surprised and embarrassed when she had what she described as a serious bout of depression and anxiety.

"Very well-meaning family friends looked at me and said, 'Aren't you just so happy, don't you just feel amazing?' And I just burst into tears because I didn't know what to say. I felt so the opposite of what their expectations were for me," Jackson said.

Saumya Dave, a psychiatrist who is the child of South Asian immigrants, was pregnant during her residency and internship. Dave had awful morning sickness, but she was chief resident at a short-staffed hospital at the time and did not want to let the other residents down. "I hadn't told anyone I was pregnant because I was in my first trimester, so I carried around a plastic bag from Fairway to throw up in so no one would know," she said.

Dave felt that both medical culture and her family's culture focused on resilience and grit. "Obviously these are qualities that are great and help in so many ways, but they can also make you want to minimize your hardships," she said. Even though as a psychiatrist she knew it was perfectly normal to not feel great all the time, she could not accept that for herself. "You can have these split selves," she said. "I remember some days being exhausted because I think I was putting on a happy face all day, and not being authentic." The performance was just another layer of stress for her.

Many women spoke of the impact of performative pregnancy on social media as something that gave them unrealistic expectations of the way their pregnancies would play out—and the pristine images projected by influencers impact women beyond national borders.

"All these beautiful images, these beautiful photo shoots with flower crowns, subconsciously led me to assume that pregnancy was easy, or that it was a beautiful process day in and day out," said Maame Adjei, who was pregnant with her first child in Accra, Ghana, when we spoke. "I'm a very analytical person, but when it comes to pregnancy, I didn't do that at all. [The influencers] kind of fooled me a little bit."

Women also felt pressured to be thin, by both those images of perfect pregnancy and the medical establishment. Mohini, a self-described fat woman with a history of disordered eating, said she felt bad during her first pregnancy because she did not carry her child in a big perfect bump, like the image of "probably a white woman, probably a married cis white woman, who weighed twelve pounds to begin with" and now walks around with her body unchanged but for her round belly, she said.

During birth especially, Mohini felt like, "No one here trusts me, who sees me as a person who can be listened to. I stopped being a wife, a daughter, a lawyer. I was a body who had a fetus in it and the fetus needed to come out."

FEELING BAD ABOUT FEELING BAD

Many women I interviewed cried while talking about their pregnancies, which were often years in the past. The word "traumatic" was used by several of them, and the experiences they described were deeply upsetting to hear about—the polar opposite of that glowing goddess they expected themselves to be.

Candace Jackson said it's still "embarrassing to talk about" the really dark thoughts she briefly experienced during her first pregnancy. "I had a night where I could barely stay alive. I felt a compulsion to do something that was physically harmful to myself."

Having that experience encouraged her to mention her mental health issues to her doctor for the first time. Before that, she had never heard of prenatal depression or anxiety, and worried she would sound ridiculous talking about it. "Would anybody even believe it?" she wondered at the time. Her family was supportive, but they are positive thinkers, and because she could not muster happy vibes, she felt phony. "You can't think your way out of anxiety," she said, and instead of getting the message to just think cheery thoughts, "what you really need is someone who can listen to your reality and not project another reality onto you."

Although most women I spoke to said that seeking help from mental health professionals was accepted in their communities, Maame Adjei said that she still has never been able to tell her mom that she has had therapy. "It's not what we know culturally" in Ghana, she said. "Maybe you talk to a family member and pray about it. We're very Christian. You talk to your mum and it's fine." Though she does say that there is a big generational difference, and that younger Ghanaians, and those who have spent time outside the country, are more accepting of getting professional mental health care.

Several women I interviewed were pregnant with their second children when we spoke in the fall of 2020. I asked them how it was different from their first pregnancy, and imagined that dealing with the pandemic would create a new kind of stress for them.

But among white-collar women who had the privilege to work from home, I was surprised to find out that they actually felt pregnancy was *less* stressful the second time around, despite coronavirus lurking around every corner.

"I feel more clear on my boundaries and what I need," said Sadie, who was two months pregnant when we spoke. "We haven't told our families. We're not really seeing them at all because of the pandemic, so they don't see that I'm sleepy and I'm nauseous." Because she doesn't see them in person, she does not have to manage the pressure of their expectations. She can be tired, barfy, and depressed, and crucially, she can get more rest.

Being able to wear comfortable clothing, avoid a commute, take naps, and stay close to a bathroom without worrying about coworkers noticing a change in their behavior is also a boon to these pregnant women. Mohini described how, during her first pregnancy, when she lived in Washington, DC, she burst into tears when a cockroach crawled on her while she was commuting on the Metro.

She tried to negotiate a more flexible working situation with her boss, but was told she did not qualify. Mohini thought her boss would be more understanding because she was also a mother, and had been on bed rest during one of her pregnancies. But her boss's attitude was "Well, I went through it, and my bootstraps were pulled up, and it's your fault if yours aren't laced yet," Mohini said.

A NATURAL EXPERIMENT, AND A VISION FOR THE FUTURE

There is some preliminary evidence from the pandemic that society's expectations of ideal motherhood—that you should be continuing to joyfully work and exercise and generally live life as if you are not pregnant—are actively harming women's health.

Several studies in different countries have shown that the coronavirus lockdowns decreased the number of premature births, possibly by as much as 20 percent. It was the perfect natural experiment; you could never create conditions like the COVID-19 lockdowns for a study by design. The effect was particularly pronounced for mothers privileged enough to work from home or not work at all.[6] This is not to argue that women shouldn't be working while they're pregnant; merely that we need to put women's health and the health of their children over the pressure to be "ideal" workers.

I wonder if we are also underestimating the stress of performing pregnancy for the world. When you are pregnant, your body becomes a topic of public conversation whether you want it to or not. I remember walking down the street near my apartment when I was seven months pregnant with my second daughter. It was a hot May day and I was wearing a fitted sundress and feeling like an overheated sea lion. A man walked by and catcalled me, yelling about my tits, which are nothing special when I'm not pregnant. It was both humiliating and a little funny, which was often the mixture of emotions I felt about my pre- and post-birth body.

Though it was 2012, I basically lived a quarantine-friendly life for the second half of my first pregnancy. During the month I spent in bed, I slept twelve to fourteen hours a day, and had sweaty, luxurious, hormone-laden naps. It wasn't all sunshine: I was still throwing up a lot. My skin was a wreck, and my hair was still embarrassingly thin. And I was still anxious. I worried the Prozac I was on was harming my baby, and I worried no one would ever consider me for a real job ever again, after I had fizzled out so quickly in my first major leadership role.

But these worries felt so much more manageable because I had the benefit of rest, medical care, and weekly talk therapy. After that month I spent prone, I started going for walks in my neighborhood when I felt up to it. I remember the first full meal I kept down—a fried chicken sandwich on a puffy potato bun that tasted like heaven.

I began to look for a few freelance assignments because I thought that if I could at least keep my name in editors' inboxes, my industry would still remember I existed, and I could begin to dig out of the hole I had made.

One of the assignments I would end up getting was a series on prenatal depression for Slate. I wrote about what happened to me, and also about what we know about mental illness during pregnancy (it turns out, not all that much). It ran when I was six months along and the experience was cathartic for the most part. It made me feel like my prenatal depression wasn't entirely my fault; there were genetic and biological components that were out of my control.

There is some evidence that women who react badly to hormonal birth control, which I always did, may be more susceptible to perinatal depression. A figure that stuck with me from my reporting is that during your first trimester of pregnancy, you're getting four hundred birth control pills' worth of progesterone a day, and by the third trimester, you are getting a thousand birth control pills' worth. No wonder I lost my damn mind.[7]

I couldn't temper the hormonal onslaught. But I do wonder if my anxiety would have been less extreme if I hadn't been so worried all the time about losing my livelihood. If I had lived in a country that gave support for women to stop working during pregnancy when they needed to, would I have been less distraught?

For example, in many European countries, taking sick leave during pregnancy is culturally normalized and financially supported. A study of around three thousand women from Norway, which has universal health care and paid sick leave, showed that three-quarters of women had taken at least one week of sick leave during their pregnancies. The median length of sick leave was eight weeks, and half of women needed between four and sixteen full weeks away from work.[8] This is what should be standard for American mothers, too.

Though part of me knew that it wasn't a moral failing to take care of my health and my baby's health, it sure felt like one, and that feeling persisted through the rest of my first pregnancy. One excellent and necessary step forward is decoupling our ideas of prenatal health and goodness. Another would be ceasing to pretend that every bit of our children's well-being is under our control from the second we conceive.

Though I knew from my reporting that stress *and* antidepressant use during pregnancy are both risk factors for premature birth and low birth weight, I went into labor four days past my due date. One silver lining of the misery of my first trimester was that I went into the birth process with zero expectations. My birth plan was: show up at Mount Sinai and leave with a (hopefully) healthy baby. I did not decide whether I wanted an epidural until I was at the hospital, though when I decided I wanted one, it could not come fast enough.

It wasn't until I was in active labor that they realized my baby was enormous. The first obstetrician overseeing me was at the end of her shift when she informed me that my baby's head had actually gone back up—which was not a thing any pregnancy book had ever prepared me for. "We're going to drain your bladder to see if that helps," she said, "but if it doesn't, you may have to have a C-section." By that point I had been in labor for almost twenty-four hours, and I did not care what happened as long as they got that baby out of me in one piece.

But then a new doctor began to attend to me. He took one look at my nethers and said that he didn't think I'd need a C-section. "You have a good pelvis. You can do this," he said. And another hour and a burst blood vessel in my right eye later, I did.

A healthy baby girl was born. All 9 pounds, 3 ounces of her. The first thing I said after she came out was "I feel so much better." As I held my hearty little bear, red-faced and squalling in my arms, I felt love, but more than that—I felt relief. And I started to think about what lay ahead.

THREE

Identity

"THIS SHOULDN'T BE ABOUT TORTURING
YOURSELF OR YOUR BABY"

In some ways, my internal adjustment to being a mother was easier than I feared it might be. Unlike many mothers I have spoken to, whose sense of self changed abruptly once their babies were born, I felt like my life had already detonated when I was pregnant. By the time my daughter was born, I had partially rebuilt myself.

What I had to get used to, though, was the way the whole world perceives you differently when you're a mother, and most of the problems I had in early motherhood came from brushing up against my culture's expectations of who I was supposed to be. I was expected to suppress any needs, desires, and unmotherly personality traits for what other people felt was "best" for the baby.

It helped that I really did feel so much better the moment the baby emerged. It was as if that scrim of darkness had been lifted off my body in the delivery room. My emotional self felt returned to me, along with my physical self. Everything flooded out of my body: pregnancy hormones, blood, water, and breastmilk.

Though I had a decent supply, I still failed at breastfeeding immediately. My daughter spent one night in the NICU—she had been grunting a little too much for the attending pediatrician's liking, and they wanted to observe her more closely to make sure there was nothing wrong with her breathing. "If we had someplace between the nursery and the NICU to put her, we'd put her there," he said to us, "but we don't."

So instead of trying to breastfeed her from her first minutes, experiencing the sainted skin-to-skin contact and letting her naturally root toward my exposed nipple, I slumped over a hospital-grade pump, exhausted and trying to figure out how all the parts worked. I pumped out some colostrum and fell asleep.

A few hours later, when I trundled down to look at her through plastic, I passed by the other intensive-care residents and felt a surge of powerful guilt. My red-cheeked, nine-pound daughter looked like another species. The NICU nurses had me hold her while they monitored us.

I had barely held a baby before I had my own. At thirty, I was the first of my close friends to have children, and this was the first baby of the new generation on both sides of our families. Thirty is dead average for college-educated women to become mothers in the United States generally,[1] but in cities like New York and San Francisco, the average is edging up to thirty-three. As the birth rate plummets overall in the United States, the only group of women who are having more first-time babies than in previous generations are women over thirty-five.[2]

Despite my inexperience, I felt fairly confident as I fed my daughter with a combination of formula and my pumped breastmilk through a bottle. After about a day in the NICU, she was moved to the nursery, and we got a dry run of caring for an infant. The nurses patiently taught us how to swaddle and change diapers. They brought the baby into our room to breastfeed, and tried to help me position her properly. But I could never get her to latch in a way that wasn't excruciatingly painful, and since the hospital-grade pump was still in my room, I switched over to that whenever I could to build up my supply, the baby's gentle breathing syncopated with the mechanical *thump-thump-thump* of the Medela.

The next morning I went to a hospital-run breastfeeding class with a lactation consultant. I remember three things from it: The low angle of the bright December light streaming through the windows and into my eyes. The Hasidic woman in my class with an elegantly long neck, a head covering, and the most regal expression on her face as she calmly breastfed her infant. And the bumbling, painful failure I experienced in the room. No matter how many hands-on adjustments I received, it still hurt beyond measure, and it started to awaken my anxiety.

Another day passed and we drove her back to our apartment. I still could not get the baby to latch right, and I was spending what felt like half my waking hours sitting in a plush rocking chair, attached to the pump. I would get up in the middle of the night to change her and feed her the bottle, put her back down, and then sit in that rocking chair listening to BBC World Service on the radio with the flanges hanging off my breasts, long enough to bleed through my pad onto the cream-colored fabric, which I then tried to scrub in the pitch-dark room.

I knew that I should breastfeed, that everyone in the hospital had encouraged me to work through the pain and discomfort. I wanted to *want to* breastfeed, to ace the first test of early motherhood.

But truly, in my deepest soul, I did not want to. I didn't want to breastfeed and I didn't want to pump. I felt like my physical self had been so drained by pregnancy—wrung of its nutrients and tossed aside like a used mop. I wanted my body back.

I tensed up just thinking about bringing my baby to my breast, knowing how badly it would hurt. I worried that there was something deeply aberrant and unmaternal about me because I felt so negative about the whole experience. I recalled the many books I had read about Queen Victoria and her wayward son, the future King Edward, that implied their relationship was damaged from the start, in part because breastfeeding him made her feel "insurmountable disgust."[3]

The fear of irrevocable damage made me keep trying. We brought in a lactation consultant at $200 an hour, and although I could get the baby to latch properly while the lactation consultant was physically holding her up to me, that was the only time we achieved a painless communion. The second the consultant left, we reverted to whatever it was we were doing incorrectly. My husband only had a week of parental leave, so very quickly after my daughter was born, I was struggling alone most of the time.

The sleeplessness involved with pumping and trying to breastfeed was exacerbating my anxiety, and it made me fear that I would tip into postpartum depression. I bought nipple shields recommended by an acquaintance, and read pages of internet comments trying to hack my breastfeeding issues. I remember waking up from a brief nap, soaked in milk, and bursting into tears at the thought of having to continue to compromise my body for another year.

And so I quit breastfeeding after two weeks.

I'm not going to relitigate the arguments for and against breastfeeding at all maternal costs because it shouldn't be an argument. It should be about letting women have agency over their own bodies, and social support either way.

I have read all the studies, and I know that formula is perfectly adequate nutrition for babies, even if it's arguably inferior to breastmilk. I also know that when you look at long-term outcomes and control for other factors, the difference between breastfed and formula-fed children is minimal.

For example, one of the best long-term studies on breastfeeding is of over thirteen thousand children in Belarus. It was a randomized, controlled study, which is quite rare in the breastfeeding literature, where most of the studies are observational. When researchers followed up with children at sixteen, they found no significant cognitive differences between babies who were exclusively breastfed for less than three months and those who were breastfed for more than three months: "We observed no benefit of a breastfeeding promotion intervention on overall neurocognitive function."[4]

Although adequate paid parental leave would help women meet their breastfeeding goals, it's worth noting that even in Sweden, where parents are entitled to 480 days of leave,[5] only 15 percent of mothers are exclusively breastfeeding at six months.[6] Just as in other aspects of mothering, falling short of either tacit or overt recommendations leads to guilt and self-recrimination. As one Swedish mother told researchers, "You get criticized if you stop breastfeeding, as if you're vain or lazy . . . and if you do it for too long it's regarded as too hippie, so you should [breastfeed] a perfect length of time in between."[7]

I understand why breastfeeding is important in some cases, especially when babies are premature, and that there is still discrimination against many who breastfeed. Low-income women, in particular, face what experts describe as "insurmountable" barriers: they rarely get paid leave, they may not have access to clean spaces or time to pump at work, and they are less likely to have flexible schedules.[8] I believe women should be supported—at work, at home, and in public spaces—in breastfeeding for as long as they want to. I think lactation consultants should be available to everyone for free.

I asked for absolution from mine, a beautiful, clog-wearing hippie. She told me: "This shouldn't be about torturing yourself or your baby." I was grateful for her pardon, but also felt squirrelly for having needed it. I think I just wanted to say I had official permission when people asked me why I wasn't nursing, because I felt like "I didn't want to" was not enough.

And lo, did they ask. An astounding number of people, upon hearing that I had recently given birth, asked me, "How is nursing going?" They asked me on my Facebook page and at parties and on the subway, and they always assumed I was doing it. I remember being scared to bottle-feed at the park for fear that someone would jump out of the bushes and shout, "Boo! Boo! Rubbish! Filth! Slime! Muck! Boo! Boo! Boo!" like that crone in *The Princess Bride*.

This is because in the upper-middle-class, Northeastern universe I orbit, breastfeeding is normative. It was the baseline expectation of what a "good" mother did. This isn't the case in all communities. The pressure to breastfeed (or to formula feed) is heavily influenced by your friends, family, and culture.[9]

In the United States, breastfeeding rates are all over the place, with the lowest rates of initiation in the Southeast. Asian infants have the highest level of breastfeeding initiation, at 92 percent, followed by white and Hispanic infants, who are breastfed at rates of around 85 percent. Non-Hispanic Black infants have the lowest rates of breastfeeding initiation, at 75 percent.[10]

Scholars such as Andrea Freeman have written about the lack of societal and governmental support for Black women breastfeeding, and the historically racist treatment of Black mothers. Enslaved women were taken from their own children to nurse white infants, and this act "required moral justification in the form of stories about black women as bad and uncaring mothers," Freeman wrote.[11]

As my friend Hanna, who told me I was out of my fucking mind, put it in a 2009 article for the *Atlantic*, the current, frenzied debate around breastfeeding takes place without any reference to its history, or its context in women's lives.

Exclusive breastfeeding "is a serious time commitment," she

wrote. "This is why, when people say that breast-feeding is 'free,' I want to hit them with a two-by-four. It's only free if a woman's time is worth nothing."[12]

Considering this serious commitment, I don't understand why we aren't framing the extremely high rates of breastfeeding initiation as a great success story in the United States. In 1972, only 22 percent of women breastfed their babies. By the time I was born, in 1982, the rate was up to 61 percent,[13] and by 2018, the rate was almost 84 percent.[14] This is incredible progress in a short amount of time: Why is our narrative that mothers aren't doing enough? Of course, it is much less expensive to shame mothers endlessly than it is to provide them with the tools that would enable them to breastfeed more easily and for longer.

Formula shouldn't be the moral flashpoint that it has become, but as Joan B. Wolf, author of *Is Breast Best?* puts it, breastfeeding "serves as a repository for numerous cultural anxieties, many of which have little to do with infant feeding."[15] Wolf calls the new identity that mothers must embody "total motherhood," which is "a moral code in which mothers are exhorted to optimize every aspect of children's lives, beginning with the womb."[16]

In this framing, if a mother's needs are in conflict with a child's needs, she is automatically supposed to sacrifice herself, even if the gains to the child may be small and poorly understood compared with the cost to the mother, which may be substantial. There is no notion of a mother-child dyad—no nuanced ideas about how a mother's mental health or well-being is also in the best interest of the baby.

Total motherhood also ignores the systemic issues, like lack of paid parental leave, poverty, and racism, that may affect a woman's choices, and render them barely "choices" at all. Everything is on you as an individual mother, the stakes of every decision are sky high, and if anything goes wrong with your kid, that's your fault.

After speaking with other mothers for this chapter, it's clear the emotional and physical costs of total motherhood are significant and aren't showing any signs of abating.

NO NEW FRIENDS

After I had my daughter, I didn't feel like my core personality traits had changed (or, as I like to put it: I'm still the same asshole I was before). Though I had read horror stories about new moms feeling ditched by their child-free friends, that wasn't my experience. Because my daughter was the first baby in our set, she was a fun novelty. My friends' wallets had not yet been exhausted by purchasing fourteen onesies a year for new additions, and so they were excited to greet her. I was thrilled to hear about lives that didn't involve projectile spit-up.

Even though I was supported by my friends at the time, I felt compelled to try to make some mom friends because that's what you were supposed to do when you had a baby. When I was still pregnant, I dutifully joined the local online December 2012 moms group to meet some.

At first I just lurked on the message board, observing the other women and their habits from an anthropological distance. They started hanging out together while we were all still pregnant. I was still sick and exhausted then, and didn't have the energy to hoist myself out of bed and into real clothes for a get-together at a local beer garden. But I felt a noxious combination of excluded and superior when the day following the outing the message board blew up with chatter about everyone's choices for baby names. *"Tree," what a dumb hippie name,* I thought to myself, while also feeling sad no one was asking about whether my husband and I had finally settled on something.

After my daughter was born, I would see pairs of other mothers walking with their babies down the windy sidewalks, laughing as they retrieved tiny socks that had blown off in January gusts, and I began to worry that I was missing out on some essential connection. So when I saw a hangout scheduled at someone's home nearby I felt I needed to give it a try.

It occurred to me, as I trudged through the late winter slush to go to my first in-person meetup with these moms, that having a child was not actually the basis of any kind of relationship. The only thing most of us had in common was that we had sex in March 2012. That fact of nature applies to billions of people, but it was supposed to be the foundation of a deep and necessary bond.

I entered the well-appointed apartment trying to find a place for my daughter's stroller. Almost everyone else had worn their baby— another thing I had tried and discarded, against the trend.

As I took off all my layers, and all the baby's layers, I felt ten sets of eyes appraising me. I stepped gingerly around the mothers and babies splayed on the furniture and on the floor and introduced myself. Everyone was friendly, but I remember almost all the conversation orbited around breastfeeding and sleeping struggles. I had given up the first, and the second wasn't really an issue, so I didn't say very much.

When the topic of work came up, it turned out I was the only person who had started back at any kind of paid employment. My bank account was getting anemic; freelancers don't get paid parental leave, and I had barely worked for the majority of my pregnancy. I started sending out pitches while the baby slept, and I was delighted to find out that my brain still worked the way I needed it to. I got enough assignments right away that it made sense for us to hire a nanny for thirty hours a week. As first-time parents, she taught us so much, and I was beyond grateful that I found someone I could trust.

I remember explaining this to the group, and instead of looking at me with admiration for getting back into the swing of things and helping to support my family, I recall them gazing at me with pity. "I just can't imagine working so soon!" I remember them saying.

Though the group was internet-based and ostensibly open to all, everyone was middle to upper middle class. Considering that some studies show a quarter of low-wage workers have to go back to work within two weeks of their children's births,[17] it's no wonder that we were the women who had the free time in the middle of the week to gather with our two-month-olds.

But their response shows the peril of the mom group, which is that they tend to have their own sets of norms. Even if you are a reluctant joiner, like me, you will feel uncomfortable about transgressing whatever the ideals might be of the women around you.

Kiah Bowers, twenty-eight, who is a mom of a three-year-old in Tampa, Florida, felt totally abandoned by a "crunchy," attachment parenting mom group when she failed to live up to their rules. "Those crunchy, natural circles, it can be very judgmental," Kiah said. "You could always be better at it than someone else, and things get pretty vicious."

Kiah is married to a woman, and she was first attracted to the "natural" parenting groups in Tampa because she thought they would be more like-minded—more diverse, and more open to gay parents like herself. She got involved with those groups when she became pregnant, and she decided she wanted to try to have a home birth.

She started out delivering at home with local midwives, but her labor stalled. "I ended up with a hospital transfer," she said. Her midwives couldn't stay with her for the birth, and when she got to the hospital, "They immediately got me on Pitocin, antibiotics, the opposite kind of birth I thought I wanted," she said. Considering it didn't go according to plan, Kiah said her birth was respectful. Her doctors and nurses "went the extra mile to consult me for another nine hours instead of doing a C-section. I was able to have a vaginal birth in hospital."

Even though she did not have the kind of birth she had dreamed of, she thought she would still be able to do all the other "natural" things recommended by the moms groups. But "almost immediately I felt dropped by the midwifery group, like oh, I failed home birth. That's your first black mark against you in the crunchy parenting circles," Kiah said.

She did not experience the ecstatic joy some women describe experiencing during breastfeeding. Kiah suffered from D-MER, or dysphoric milk ejection reflex. That's when breastfeeding women experience "an abrupt emotional 'drop'" just before milk is released, which may manifest as self-loathing, anxiety, depression, or anger.[18]

Kiah breastfed her baby for a year despite this emotional disturbance. "I definitely think I pressured myself into doing it a lot longer because I had spent so long with that rhetoric of 'of course breastfeeding is best, and of course you messed up home birth, of course you need to breastfeed,'" she said. Baby wearing was another source of anxiety; her baby hated to be worn.

"I would feel this extreme guilt for putting my baby in a stroller to walk around Target," she said, because so many people were telling her if she didn't wear her baby, the child would be maladapted in some way. Kiah is a research scientist, and she knew there wasn't evidence showing her kid would be damaged if she used a stroller, but she found the peer pressure to be excessive.

Kiah also thinks that being a young, queer parent amps up the pressure she felt, and continues to feel to some extent. There's a context of wanting to prove to the world that she and her wife can parent as well as older, wealthier, heterosexual parents who are the cultural norm, she said.

Ultimately, her wife convinced her to be easier on herself. She pumped and would let her wife take some of the nighttime feedings so she could sleep. "I felt I couldn't tell anyone in my group that I was doing it," she said. "I'm a scientist and had a medicalized traumatic conception and I tried to overcompensate by being the earth mother."

She feels cynical about the whole thing, and now that she and her wife are trying for their second baby, they are trying to get an in-person LGBTQ parenting group off the ground, though it's been tough with COVID-19 still lingering.[19]

CREATING A NECESSARY LIFELINE

This is not to say that all mom groups are judgmental and oppressive. Many women I talked to genuinely felt that online connections had saved their lives through the most difficult parts of parenting, and got them through some of the worst moments they had ever experienced. In particular, I heard from several moms who had newborns in the NICU, who struggled to conceive, or who experienced miscarriage or stillbirth and found online connections were essential.

Wynter Mitchell-Rohrbaugh, forty-one, a content strategist in Los Angeles, had to terminate three very wanted pregnancies for medical reasons, an experience she described as heartbreaking and lonely. "I felt such a deep sense of failure and fear, and immediately I started wondering if there's something wrong with me," she said. The self-blame started running through her head: Why did we wait so long to have kids? Why did I focus on work for so many years? Does my husband secretly think I am less of a woman because this is happening?

She said that she loves the groups that she is in for women experiencing the kinds of losses she is going through—one of the communities is on Discord, and it is heavily moderated and anonymous. Wynter sometimes finds it "easier to communicate with these women I don't know than with people I'm friends with." They provide comfort and understanding, and in her words, they don't bullshit her. Sometimes her friends will try to tell her everything is going to be okay, and after what she's been through, she knows that sometimes it's not.[20]

Kari Cobham, thirty-nine, had a rough second pregnancy, which she didn't expect. Her pregnancy with her older child, a girl, had been relatively easy, she said. "I was expecting the second pregnancy would be easy, and it was the opposite." She joined a Facebook group for high-risk pregnancies, and, after her son was born early and needed to spend time in the NICU, she joined a Facebook group for NICU moms.

"There were people going through the same experience at the same time," she said. "The group was really helpful in helping me navigate the language of the NICU." They understood why Kari was so upset when the NICU nurse had given her son his first bath because it was a reminder of how many milestones she had to miss, and how different her experience was this time around. She immediately "burst into tears" when she found out, she said.

The group helped her figure out what to say to the nurses without offending them; she knew they were just doing their jobs, but it still hurt. And the group was a font of helpful information around navigating insurance and other practical issues that can feel overwhelming when you've just given birth and you're worried about your newborn.

On the other hand, Kari, a journalist, has found the Facebook groups for her suburban Atlanta community to be unwelcoming. Kari is Black and East Indian, and an immigrant from Trinidad and Tobago. She said in her local groups there is an assumption that you are in a two-parent household and you are probably financially comfortable, and the admins don't take constructive feedback very well.

To have a more nourishing community of moms to sustain her, Kari cofounded her own Facebook group for journalist moms in 2016. She and her cofounder came up with a list of ground rules, which are constantly evolving, that they felt would foster inclusion for many different kinds of parents.

For example, "A mom reached out to us and said that they felt like they'd seen a couple of instances where ableist language was being used. They found it offensive and was going to leave the group if it didn't change," Kari said. So she and her cofounder did research and asked for specific examples. It led to them drafting some new rules and making language recommendations.[21]

It took years for me to find communities of mom friends in person and online, and the key for me was that I made these relationships organically and through shared interests beyond our kids. I made a handful of friends through my older daughter's first preschool class, with whom I am still close even though our kids go to different schools now.

I also have a years-long WhatsApp chat with eight other moms who were brought together by the internet, some of whom I have never met in person. That chat provides me daily support, humor, and visibility that are vital to my emotional well-being. Though the women in my chat have different life circumstances and live in different parts of the country, we have a shared sensibility and attitude toward parenting. It helps that we never shame each other, and that we talk about everything in our lives: work, friends, spouses, family, and the entire slate of Bravo programming. We are allowed to be full people with each other, and not just an appendage of our children.

"THE MOST AMAZING VERSION OF MYSELF"

Nearly every woman I spoke to for this chapter used the same word to describe how they felt about their inability to subsume themself fully into early motherhood: "guilty."

They felt guilty for continuing to work and leaving their children in the care of others, and they felt guilty about leaving work and feeling lost, or never having a job they felt was a career in the first place. They felt guilty about having postpartum depression, and they felt guilty about not living up to the perfectly heteronormative, naturalistic, and pristine ideals of their communities. Even when they were deeply aware of the flaws in society's ideals, those ideals got in their heads.

They expected motherhood to be completely transformative, and felt bad about themselves when it was not metamorphic. "The minute he was delivered, I thought I was going to magically be the most amazing version of myself. The angelic Angela," said Angela Hatem, forty-three, who is a single mom to a two-and-a-half-year-old son in Indianapolis, Indiana.[22] In her book, *Mom: The Transformation of Motherhood in Modern America*, Rebecca Jo Plant describes the expectations that Angela had as being at least a hundred years old in American culture. "Mother love . . . had the capacity to transform and redeem: it could turn a shallow and vapid woman into a noble character."[23]

Because Angela went through several rounds of IVF to have her baby, she felt especially guilty for not being magically transformed by motherhood. She said she had gotten to a point where she "just begged God, please, please, all I want is a baby, I'll never want for anything again." She also feels additional pressure as a single mom. "I don't want anyone to think he's going to have less because he doesn't have a father," she said.

A woman I will call Jiah,[24] who is thirty-seven, also went through IVF to conceive her daughter, who is now two. When she was going through IVF and had a miscarriage, but before she had a successful pregnancy, she felt like she "wasn't trying hard enough" because she didn't know if she was willing to continue to put her body, her marriage, her sanity, and her finances through endless rounds of fertility treatment. When she finally did get pregnant with her child, she felt like any bad feelings she had during pregnancy and postpartum were supposed to be pushed down because "your body and comfort and feelings shouldn't matter if you're in this holy journey to become a mother."

Jiah grew up in South Korea and in California, and said that while her own mom stayed home, she "definitely mourned having to give up her career. But at the same time, she used to be very big on 'mothers should stay at home with their kids till they're three,' or at least until they're one."

Her mother is horrified at the lack of paid leave and other benefits afforded to parents in the United States. Jiah and her husband do not have local family support, and since they had their daughter during the pandemic, they have been juggling childcare and working from home without any outside help.

Although she feels lucky that she is able to stay home and keep her job, "If you're trying to juggle everything, it feels like it's a struggle," Jiah said. "Everyone else tells you, 'you should really enjoy this time, it's so precious.' But have they tried working forty-five hours a week with a five-month-old baby clamoring for their attention?"

Breen Nolan Schoen, thirty-seven, who lives in Portland, Oregon, with her three-and-a-half-year-old daughter, became a stay-at-home mom, but not by choice. "I left a career I spent ten years building because I couldn't handle the pressure of both," she wrote to me. "It's been almost two years and my husband has continued to climb the ladder while I'm taking care of our daughter in peanut-butter-stained sweatpants. One Zoloft at a time."

Breen had severe postpartum depression and anxiety, which led to suicidal ideation; at her worst moment she threatened to jump out of a moving car. She said that her job as an executive in a male-dominated field was her whole identity before she had a child. Breen had that "supermom" vision of herself as a new mom, "wearing a nice silk blouse and carrying my pumping stuff and just getting shit done." Instead, she was so anxious she couldn't sleep, she worried about her daughter's well-being all the time, and found her life totally impossible to maintain.

She ended up leaving her job and is still struggling with her sense of identity. She has a bit of childcare now, but doesn't quite know what to do with herself even when she has an hour or two to spare. "It's hard to differentiate what I need to do and what I want to do, and sometimes it's hard to figure out and I just do nothing," Breen said.[25]

"I EXPECTED TO JUMP RIGHT INTO THAT WIFE AND MOTHER ROLE"

Angela, Jiah, and Breen did not mention the role of religion in their conceptions of ideal motherhood. But for Janan Graham-Russell, thirty-two, who is mother to a five-year-old and an eighteen-month-old in Salt Lake City, much of the pressure she felt was from fellow Mormons and their cultural norms. "I remember when I had my first kid, there was some apprehension (internal and external) about how I would 'mother' and continue to go to grad school/get my PhD," Janan said. "Women working outside the home is the exception, not the rule within Mormon culture."[26]

Janan was not raised Mormon—she joined the church eleven years ago because she liked the religion's emphasis on family, and the idea that families could be together forever. But with that family focus comes the always implicit, and sometimes explicit, message that spiritually motherhood is "the most important job that a woman has ever had, and that leaves out single women, and persons who are unable to carry for whatever reason," she said.

Janan is also a Black woman who was raised by a single mom, and she can feel alienated from the Mormon ideal because "it's not just any motherhood, it's a specific look of motherhood. It's perfect hair, it's often white women," portraying "a very constructed, racially and economically uniform version of motherhood that we see on Instagram."

She added, "As a Black woman, I didn't feel like I had the same opportunities to focus on motherhood and get back into my career at a later time. Nor did I believe that motherhood was some divine calling, which is often emphasized in Mormonism." She feels like she is in a better place now with her identity than she was when she initially became a mother in her twenties, but "those first few years were rough."

Carmen C., thirty-four, who is the mom of a toddler in Colorado, was raised in an Italian Catholic household, and her dad was in the army. She described the two conservative cultures together as a "toxic combination" for her. "You marry your spouse—typically a hetero couple—and then you are married to the career."

"Military spouses don't often have careers because of the frequent moving—it doesn't allow for that—so naturally you fall back on being a stay-at-home mom," she said.[27] "I don't think I ever made an effort in crafting an identity because I didn't expect to have one. I expected to jump right into that wife and mother role."

She is a military wife herself, and it's been very difficult for her to accept that she doesn't want to be a full-time mom. Carmen said it took her a year of therapy to get comfortable with sending her kids to day care, and now she is working part time. "I would talk to my parents or my mom, and they would say something like, 'sacrifice Carmen, sacrifice.'" Though her husband is very supportive of her working, it's tough to get over all the messages she has internalized over the years.

BEST-LAID PLANS

Myra Jones-Taylor, forty-six, the mom of two teenagers and the chief policy impact officer of the Urban Institute, a nonprofit research organization, said that she was aware of the unreasonable demands of ideal motherhood from day one, and she knew she wanted to push back against them. "I'm a Black woman in this world, and I was going to resist this idea that I had to give up everything to be an effective mother," she said.[28] As she put it, beautifully: she rejects the notion that "your child's wholeness meant you were less than whole."

Myra is the only person I talked to who had her husband read *The Second Shift*—the sociologist Arlie Russell Hochschild's book about the disproportionate burden of housework and childcare on mothers—years before they were married and had kids. In college "I would read parts out to him aloud, and quiz him where he stood on this topic," she said.

She made sure that childcare and domestic tasks were divided equally between her and her husband from the beginning, so her husband knew the patterns of their daughter's night wakings as well as she did. Once her children were old enough, she made sure they were as independent as possible so she and her husband weren't stuck doing laundry that their teens were perfectly capable of doing themselves.

But still, she has to do extra labor as a mother to signal to the world that her spouse is just as much a parent as she is. For example, Myra and her husband divide the children's health care: she manages the pediatrician visits, and he manages the dentist.

And yet the dentist kept calling her to set up appointments, not her husband. "I had to coach them," she said, to get them to stop calling her. She had to tell them over and over again: I don't make these appointments and I don't know his work schedule. Often, even if we know our own boundaries and set them, as Myra does, maintaining them takes extra time and work as we push against society's expectations.

It doesn't have to be this way. There is no question that becoming a parent is a monumental life change, and that many mothers will need time to adapt to this new facet of their identity. Fathers experience a profound identity shift as well, but society is not as invested in scrutinizing their behavior as deeply, and they are still applauded for doing mundane things like taking their kids to the grocery store without extra help.

But we can accept this maternal identity shift without requiring that it become the most important and only part of a woman's selfhood. We can also expand the vision of what a "good" mother is and does.

In the United States, where there is so little support for parents both financially and culturally, there is additional pressure to make motherhood the core of who you are, because keeping up an identity outside of "mother" takes countless extra steps, hours, and burdens both financial and emotional.

If you need or want to keep working, you have to fight for paid leave. You have to spend hours figuring out childcare and worrying that the childcare will disappear. You have to worry about other people's judgment for whatever way you're feeding your children, or for having a toddler who acts like a normal toddler in a restaurant or on a plane. If I read one more story about parents handing out goody bags of candy to other passengers on the plane as a pre-apology for existing, I'm going to lose my mind.

When we are forced to spend so much time, energy, and money worrying about these basics of our children's lives, it can put us in a defensive crouch. It isolates us because we feel like we are hacking the path forward without support. It can make us unempathetic to other parents and oblivious to our community because we are completely exhausted.

Nations where parents aren't categorized as "other" so aggressively have much better outcomes for everyone. When sociologists compared happiness levels of parents and nonparents in twenty-two countries, they found that parents in the United States were comparatively the most miserable. The authors found that "more generous family policies, particularly paid time off and child-care subsidies, are associated with smaller disparities in happiness between parents and nonparents. Moreover, the policies that augment parental happiness do not reduce the happiness of nonparents."[29]

Caitlyn Collins, a sociologist who interviewed 135 working moms in the United States, Italy, Germany, and Sweden for her 2019 book, *Making Motherhood Work*, wrote in the *Atlantic* that the American mothers she interviewed were much more likely to cite expert views when she asked them about the definition of a "good mother."

> They routinely recited the views of experts they had gleaned from books, articles, podcasts, classes, listservs, blogs, and message boards—but a personal definition rarely followed.
>
> But the European women I spoke with rarely invoked expert views, instead talking about traits they wanted to instill in their children (stability, independence, kindness) and wanting them to feel safe and loved. Take Sara, a mom in Sweden: When I asked her what being a good mother meant, she told me, "Having time with them. I think that's the most important part. Yeah, just being with them."[30]

If the bar for "good mother" was that your children felt safe and loved, it would be a much less stressful and soul-crushing proposition than our current American standards. It would certainly take up a lot less brain space. As Collins continues: "Though women in the United States are constantly told that they can have a successful career and a rewarding family life, with next to no work-family policies to support them, 'having it all' is mostly a pipe dream. In essence, mothers are encouraged to reach for the stars while wearing strait-jackets."[31]

I felt that straitjacket tighten as we started thinking about a second child. I was very happy freelancing—possibly the happiest I have ever been professionally. I probably worked forty hours a week, but because it was for a variety of publications, I could mold it around my daughter's schedule. We didn't have to pay for full-time child-care, partially because I would work after my daughter was asleep at night, and partially because my parents, who were retired, came every Friday to spend time with me and my kid, an arrangement we all benefited from immensely.

Right after my first difficult pregnancy, I thought I was going to be one and done—I couldn't imagine putting my mind or body through that again. But when my daughter was eighteen months old, I started feeling open to another child. That desire was not rational, and I can't explain it even to myself.

We started trying for our second around my baby's second birthday. I got pregnant immediately, and lost that pregnancy late in my first trimester. The fetus had something called Turner syndrome, which is a chromosomal abnormality. My obstetrician told me it was a "good" miscarriage, as in, a fluke, totally beyond my control, and I wasn't at any additional risk of this particular abnormality happening again. This both comforted me and made me furious.

After the loss, we tried again for a few months, but when I didn't get pregnant three months in a row, I found the whole process too depressing and wanted to stop for a bit. I had just turned thirty-three, and tests confirmed I had a lot of eggs, so we didn't have to be in a big rush, medically speaking.

We also realized that to pay for a second child and remain in New York City, I would have to go back to a staff job. I didn't want a disastrous repeat of my first pregnancy, when I got sick shortly after starting a new job, so we paused our efforts until I had a chance to start the new gig and feel somewhat secure. I thought if I just planned well enough I could prevent more career upheaval. But if I had learned anything from my experience of working motherhood, it should have been clear that plans can only take you so far.

FOUR

Work

MY "WHITE GUY BEARD"

There's a way in which even places that have a lot of the things a working mother would love to have—flexibility, a good salary, engaging and ever-changing projects—can still reinforce subtle and sometimes painful gender dynamics. The job I had when I got pregnant with my second daughter, as the editor in chief of a start-up publication, was overall a positive one for me. I still have warm relationships with the people I worked with, even though, in retrospect, they sometimes inadvertently made comments or were part of situations that made me feel less than empowered.

One particular conflicted moment that sticks with me occurred when I was seven months pregnant with my second daughter. I was pacing in the cobblestone street outside my apartment, yelling at the CEO over the phone, "I'm not your secretary! It's not my job to respond to emails you haven't answered!"

By that point, about a year into the company's existence, I was getting cc'd on emails fairly often that he hadn't responded to. These were business-related emails with questions I couldn't answer, since

I didn't manage the business side. But clients would copy me because they knew I would get back to them promptly, and do the work of texting or calling the CEO to make sure he finally wrote back.

I had been asking him for months to either get a part-time assistant or just . . . answer his own email in a timely manner, to no avail. As the arrival of my baby neared, and we were trying to close an advertorial project that would bring in a huge chunk of money, I cracked.

Most of the time, our relationship was a good one. He is kind and funny and well-meaning. I remember the first meeting I had with him. My older daughter was about two and a half, and it was a few months after my miscarriage. The CEO and I had a very chatty and creatively productive breakfast at a rustic Italian restaurant with exposed brick walls.

Though this goes against all the career advice I have ever read, I was transparent about my desire to have a second child. My honesty was a calculated risk. Because my experience during my first pregnancy was so traumatizing, I felt I needed to lay my cards on the table. I figured if they didn't want someone who had a life outside of work, this would be a bad fit for all of us.

It had taken three full years for me to build back my career to the point where I would even be considered for a role like this. I had hustled to get freelance writing and editing assignments from all sorts of outlets.

Yet I still felt like I was damaged goods. I had interviewed for more corporate jobs around the time I was interviewing for this one, and I had not received any reasonable offers. I could only guess that my medical mishap—or possibly being a mom, in general—was to blame.

The CEO's response was perfect, something along the lines of, "It's not shocking to me that you might want to have another baby. We can work with that." The start-up's attitude was incredibly progressive in terms of flexibility, too. Since the founders and the CEO would be in another city much of the time, they weren't strict about my in-office working hours. As long as I was getting my work done and managing my team appropriately, they didn't care if I put in long hours of face time. They also found office space that was an easy commute for me.

The money was pretty good; even though I wasn't getting a 401(k), I would still be earning a lot more than I was freelancing, and it was enough to support another kid without upending our lives. Because I could be on my husband's health insurance, I could take a risk and be part of a tiny start-up that might offer great rewards down the line.

I felt so lucky to be getting a fresh start. And that's really what the first few months before we launched the publication felt like: a new beginning for me at work. I got to hire a team of fantastic, brilliant women, who were among the most creative people I have ever collaborated with. The founders, also women, were supportive and had impressive big-picture ideas, while also giving us creative freedom.

We sat in a rented office space above a yuppie food court and talked about the dream writers and illustrators we wanted to commission. We created the structure and consulted on the branding for the publication and the CEO brought me into conversations about the business side of media. It was generous of him, and it was a skill I felt would serve me well.

The CEO was in charge of getting us funding and advertising. It was a running joke that he served as the "white guy beard" for all of us in meetings with the money people, most of whom were also middle-aged white guys. The founders were putting their own money into the publication to start, a situation that was not sustainable, so we were seeking investment from other media companies.

I'm not sure what was more depressing: the fact that men mostly held the purse strings for women's media investments, or that I did need him in those rooms to be taken seriously by the suits and their editorial counterparts, though he rarely wore anything fancier than jeans and sneakers, while I'd be sitting next to him in full makeup and heels.

I recall one encounter with an executive at a company that ended up investing in our publication. We had come into their office for an advertising presentation. I was just starting to show my second pregnancy, and he pointed to my stomach and said, "Is it mine?"

The conversation devolved from there. After I laughed off the comment, he proceeded to tell me, in far too intimate detail, about his wife's unmedicated home births. He said something to me along the lines of, "Are you woman enough to have a home birth?" and again, I deflected.

I'm not even sure if those exchanges were meant to be sexual, as much as they were meant to make me uncomfortable, and reify the power imbalance between us. I remember our CEO getting him off my back in that conversation and, in the aftermath, acknowledging what had happened was not okay. For that I was grateful.

"THE WORLD TURNS TO WOMEN FOR MOTHERING"

My husband and I started trying for our second a month after the product launched. The publication was successful out of the gate: we had hundreds of thousands of subscribers almost immediately and a mountain of positive buzz.

I hadn't gone off Prozac since my first pregnancy, and I hoped it would be enough to keep me from cratering my life this time around. I had my older daughter to care for, and though my husband was a full partner in parenting, I knew I still had to show up for her. I couldn't spend months in bed if I could possibly help it. I also couldn't stomach the financial hit we would take if I lost this job.

I started throwing up when I was precisely six weeks pregnant;

I remember it was a Saturday, and I turned to my husband and said: "I can't live like this again." I called my obstetrician and he prescribed Diclegis, a drug that hadn't yet been approved for morning sickness[1] when I was pregnant with my older daughter.

I knew the history of Thalidomide, a morning-sickness drug, popular in the 1950s and early 1960s, that caused serious birth defects in at least ten thousand children around the world, and an unknown number of miscarriages.[2]

Thalidomide had never been approved by the FDA for use in pregnant women, but that did not stop doctors from prescribing it off-label to assuage nausea and vomiting during pregnancy.[3] Pregnant women used it as a sedative and for headache relief, too, and one Minnesota woman was told it was "safer than Alka-Seltzer."[4]

The Thalidomide disaster inspired legislation intended to prevent another similar tragedy,[5] and though I still felt uneasy about taking both the Prozac and Diclegis, I trusted my obstetrician, who was not concerned. As with almost all drugs taken during pregnancy, a risk analysis has to be done, which basically means: Is the potential damage a drug might do greater than the benefit to the mother?

Because my morning sickness was so severe, I had to accept that I needed this medication desperately, and that there were risks to both me and the baby if I didn't take any medication at all. I read the studies on Diclegis, and the risk profile looked good. Even though it felt selfish on some level to be putting my own physical needs above a hazy, inchoate fear of harm to my baby, I knew I couldn't go through the same ordeal I went through with my older daughter.

I started taking the Diclegis that Monday, and I stopped vomiting entirely. I was still nauseated all day, every day, and I was exhausted—along with typical first trimester exhaustion, sleepiness is a common side effect of the medication. But since I wasn't throwing up constantly, that felt like a win.

I had grown quite close to the two women who worked with me at our Brooklyn office, and I told them I was pregnant when I was about eight weeks along. I kept having to lie down on our couch in the middle of the day, and I felt it was easier to just be honest with them. They were both lovely about it. They asked how I was feeling all the time and seemed genuinely excited about my having a baby. I tried my best to be a supportive, kind, and competent leader for them, even on my sickest days. I hope I succeeded.

With the CEO and the founders thousands of miles away most of the time, I was able to hide my pregnancy until the very end of my first trimester. I didn't miss deadlines and was on time to every meeting, and since I could work from home on days I felt really crummy without them necessarily knowing about it, I could manage my symptoms.

When I finally told the founders about my pregnancy, they kvelled, and didn't seem concerned about my ability to do the job. The CEO was also mostly sympathetic; when he visited New York early in my second trimester, he noticed that I wasn't eating much lunch, and I told him honestly that I still felt nauseated all the time and didn't have much of an appetite. His response included making a comment about how bad he felt for me. But he also said he was glad there was a reason why I had been so harsh lately.

For all the ways my home life was supported by my company—I could be there to pick up my daughter from preschool aftercare almost every day—my relationship with the CEO sometimes felt unfair in a gendered way. I was an executive, and yet I had to act as a support system.

It wasn't just the email, though, that chafed. I kept having to apologize for his lack of responsiveness and figure out how to nudge him into responding. I tried to do it with pleasant requests, then with jokes, and then, finally, by yelling at him. Yelling was the only thing that ended up working, though it ultimately made him resent me. He'd do better for a few weeks, and then he would go back to his old habits.

Relatedly, I also had to smooth over his miscommunications with other members of our staff, and laugh off things I didn't always find funny. On a text thread with my coworkers the day after my second daughter was born, I told them that I was feeling great, and I was so happy that I never had to be pregnant again. While my other coworkers laughed and sent heart emojis, the CEO joked, "Ha. Can we put that in your contract?" I don't think he meant it to be cruel, and we had such a jokey relationship to begin with. But it was just twenty-four hours after I had given birth, I was exhausted, and it made me feel uneasy.

In her oft-cited 1983 book, *The Managed Heart*, the sociologist Arlie Russell Hochschild explains precisely the gendered roles the CEO and I were playing. It's not only embarrassing to be such a cliché, it's also a real bummer that a book originally published when I was an infant is still so relevant today.

The Managed Heart is best known for popularizing the term "emotional labor." Though at this point the term is so far removed from its original context that it is misused to mean "anything that a woman does," Hochschild's original definition is about emotional management as part of paid work. "While you may also be doing physical labor and mental labor, you are crucially being hired and monitored for your capacity to manage and produce a feeling," Hochschild explained in an interview with the *Atlantic* in 2018.[6]

Men do emotional labor, too, but it tends to be of a different sort. According to Hochschild, "Women are more likely to be presented with the task of mastering anger and aggression in the service of 'being nice.' To men, the socially assigned task of aggressing against those that break rules of various sorts creates the private task of mastering fear and vulnerability."[7] Which is to say, when the CEO was called to defend my honor with the investor, and generally act as my "male beard" in meetings where we were asking for large sums of money.

Though this dynamic applies to everyone regardless of parental status, part of the reason it is so widespread is that women are subconsciously categorized as mothers, Hochschild argues. "Women in general are asked to look out for psychological needs more than men are. The world turns to women for mothering, and this fact silently attaches itself to many a job description."[8]

If a woman transgresses an invisible boundary of "niceness," she can often expect punishment or pushback. I probably did speak harshly to the CEO in my early pregnancy; I was exhausted and felt ill, and didn't have the energy to slap a smile on my face when I needed something.

THE FUNDAMENTAL CONFLICT FOR CAREGIVERS AT WORK

Despite my high status at the company, and my genuinely positive and happy relationships with my coworkers, I could not escape the deeply ingrained dynamics around mothers at work. As mentioned earlier, Joan Williams, the director of the Center for WorkLife Law at UC Hastings, described the fundamental conflict for caregivers at work as the ideal worker versus the ideal mother. In her book *Unbending Gender: Why Family and Work Conflict and What to Do About It*, Williams describes the gender system of American domesticity as having two defining characteristics:

> The first is its organization of market work around the ideal of a worker who works full time and overtime and takes little or no time off for childbearing or child rearing. Though this ideal-worker norm

does not define all jobs today, it defines the good ones: full-time blue-collar jobs in the working-class context, and high-level executive and professional jobs for the middle class and above. When work is structured in this way, caregivers often cannot perform as ideal workers. Their inability to do so gives rise to domesticity's second defining characteristic: its system of providing for caregiving by marginalizing the caregivers, thereby cutting them off from most of the social roles that offer responsibility and authority.[9]

As Williams points out, the patterns of the ideal worker are organized around the traditional life patterns of men who have spouses occupying the home front. The fact that I was able to be at an executive level and have the flexibility to manage a difficult pregnancy makes me extraordinarily lucky as an American worker.

Statistically speaking, white women are more likely to have this kind of workplace flexibility than Black women. According to a report by Jocelyn Frye of the Center for American Progress, "Black women's labor participation rate is higher than the rate for all other women, yet black women remain less likely than their white counterparts to occupy higher-level jobs that offer better benefits, greater mobility, and economic stability."[10]

On top of this lack of access to higher-level jobs, middle- and upper-middle-class women who are not white encounter a host of racial stereotypes on top of negative assumptions around mothers' commitment to work. Dawn Marie Dow, a sociologist, shows that Black mothers in particular face twin stereotypes of the "welfare queen" and "the strong Black woman," and these stereotypes impact the decisions they make around work and family.

Dow interviewed sixty Black women in the Bay Area whose household incomes were between $50,000 and $300,000. Dow found that her interview subjects felt they needed strategies to "overcome assumptions that they are poor, single mothers on welfare or, alternatively, are self-reliant and resilient caregivers who do not need help."

These women had to navigate these stereotypes both at home and at work, and they talked about feeling excluded at predominantly white "mommy and me groups," along with additional self-presentation pressures that white women do not encounter.

Rebecca, a widow and mother of one child, felt these pressures intensely. "I think people need to know [being an African American middle-class mother] is hard," Rebecca told Dow. "It is not an easy thing because, not only are we tackling being a middle-class mom, but we are tackling the issue of race . . . I know I have woken up and thought, 'Can I just be me with no additional stuff?' . . . Why should I have to do stuff when white women don't? Maybe I just wanted to wear my yoga pants to work today, but realistically as a black woman they think, 'Oh, she is just lazy.'"[11]

For low-income women, the experience of integrating work and motherhood is even more difficult, and often cruel. Ninety-three percent of full-time workers in the bottom quarter of wage earners do not have access to paid parental leave, and 40 percent of all workers do not even have access to unpaid leave through the Family and Medical Leave Act. This lack of support for new moms leads to a quarter of them going back to work when their bodies are still healing from delivery and they are exhausted from sleeplessness.[12]

In 2014, Jodi Kantor told the story of Jannette Navarro, a single mom and retail and food service worker, in the *New York Times*. Jannette's "take-home pay rarely topped $400 to $500 every two weeks," but the even bigger problem for Jannette was that "she rarely learned her schedule more than three days before the start of a workweek, plunging her into urgent logistical puzzles" over who would watch her four-year-old son, Gavin.[13]

Jannette was at the mercy of what's called "just in time" scheduling. That's when companies use data about consumer demand to shape work schedules. Practically, this means that 20 percent of workers don't know their work hours until a week *or less* in advance. "You're waiting on your job to control your life," Jannette said.

For moms who need to arrange childcare, this kind of scheduling is a nightmare. "Young children of U.S. food and retail workers subject to last-minute scheduling go an average of fifteen days per year without childcare or supervision, compared to nine days for those who are not subject to last-minute scheduling,"[14] according to a report from the Brookings Institution.

There is evidence that this kind of scheduling, which also includes "clopening" shifts, where a worker must close a business late in the evening and then return to open it the next morning, leads to greater family conflict and a higher risk of food and housing instability, and Hispanic and Latino workers are particularly likely to be subject to this kind of last-minute scheduling, the report notes.

MORE MOTHERS WORK THAN DON'T. AMERICA DOESN'T APPROVE.

Though 71 percent of mothers with children under eighteen were in the labor force in 2020[15]—a year in which more than a million mothers were pushed out of the labor force to care for children who were home from school and day care because of the pandemic[16]— American society still does not feel fully comfortable with the idea of mothers, particularly mothers of young children, working for pay. At the same time, the hard work of caretaking is devalued at every turn, leaving many mothers feeling conflicted and guilty whether they work for pay or not.

According to a Pew study of 4,602 American adults, 59 percent believe that children with two parents are better off when a parent stays home, rather than both parents working.[17] Though older Americans are more likely to believe children are better off with a parent at home, a majority of eighteen- to twenty-nine-year-olds believe it, too. And when they say "parent," many more Americans believe that children are better off with their mothers at home, as 45 percent say it's better when the mother does not work for pay, compared with just 2 percent who say it's better when the father does not work for pay.

Only 16 percent of Americans believe that it is "ideal" for children to have a mother who works full time. Though interestingly, more Americans believe that it's better for mothers of young children to work part time than not at all.[18] And certainly, I understand the appeal: I would love to be able to work fewer hours and have more time to live my life. But there are very few "good" jobs, as Williams describes them—with benefits, with potential for advancement— that make room for part-time workers.

These conflicting feelings about moms who work for pay might explain how we got to the current, quixotic vision of the "ideal" working mother: a woman who is usually white and Christian, making scads of money off a business she runs out of her home, preferably something that incorporates and does not seem to interfere with her role as a mother. If she employs any domestic workers, they tend to be hidden from public view. And she may be already swimming in generational wealth as it is.

Think Ree Drummond of "The Pioneer Woman," one of the original momfluencers, who homeschooled her four children while creating a domestic empire on her immense cattle ranch in Pawhuska, Oklahoma. One of Drummond's hands portrays herself as just a regular mom, living the rural life, homeschooling her kids while trying to eke out time to share her recipes with us.

Meanwhile, Drummond's other hand waves away the fact that her husband's family is one of the top one hundred landowners in the United States: as of 2016, the Drummond Family owned 433,000 acres in Oklahoma and Kansas.[19]

In a *New Yorker* profile of Drummond in 2011, Amanda For-tini describes the Pioneer Woman's shtick this way:

> The Pioneer Woman is like an artifact from a more wholesome era: Ozzie and Harriet on a ranch. Even the graphics look vintage—flowers and filigreed letters in the muted colors of an antique map. There is no serious conflict, no controversy, no cynicism, no snark. Drummond doesn't discuss politics or engage in cultural crit-icism; she doesn't even gossip. Whole continents of contemporary worry go unmentioned: this is a universe free from credit-card debt, toxins, "work-life balance," and marital strife. The blog provides an escape from the viperous forces elsewhere on the Internet. De-pending on your circumstances and your disposition, the relentless good cheer can seem either admirable or annoying.[20]

This is not to pick on the Pioneer Woman specifically—I love her roasted Greek salad recipe![21] But this particular vision of combining work and caretaking, which is repeated by an endless number of sub–Pioneer Woman influencers on social media over the past two decades, making pesto eggs inside an enormous, spotless kitchen, is so beyond the wildest fantasies of the average American parent as to be absurd.

The work that goes on inside the home—caring for family mem-bers and doing domestic labor—makes the entire world function, and can be more emotionally and physically exhausting than paid work. And yet no matter how women spend their days, they cannot shed the role of "mother" without being punished.

An entire body of research shows that mothers still "fare worse in the labor market" than men or women without children—which so-ciologists call "the motherhood penalty."[22] According to Shelley Cor-rell, a sociologist and preeminent researcher on the topic, mothers earn an estimated 5 to 7 percent lower wages per child. Experiments have shown that mothers are *100 percent* less likely (not a typo) to receive a callback for an advertised job; they are significantly less likely to be recommended for hiring; and if they are recommended for hiring, they're offered $11,000 lower salaries than women without children who have the same qualifications.[23]

The reason middle- and upper-class professional women are penalized when they have children is because of those same deeply held beliefs about the way mothers should behave that Arlie Hochschild identified forty years ago: mothers are supposed to be warm and nurturing, and to have professional success in white-collar fields, you are supposed to be aggressive and competent—qualities that are unconsciously seen as masculine.

And here's yet another trap: Mothers in professional fields tend to be seen as less competent and less committed. But if they act in ways that are perceived to be masculine, for example, they are considered "cold," and while they are seen as more competent, they are also penalized for being unlikable.[24]

Even in dual-income, middle-class families, the motherhood penalty may be enough to sink them into bankruptcy if a spouse loses their job or someone in their family has an expensive medical catastrophe. As Elizabeth Warren and her daughter Amelia Warren Tyagi point out in *The Two-Income Trap, Why Middle-Class Parents Are Going Broke*, "Having a child is now the single best predictor that a woman will end up in financial collapse."[25]

Working-class mothers are often forced to make unimaginable decisions between their work and their children. Though there is not consensus among experts about the severity of welfare reform's impact in the 1990s, many believe that single mothers have been pushed into low-paying jobs where they still struggle to make ends meet, without available high-quality childcare support to back them up.[26]

As of 2019, only one in seven low-income children eligible for childcare assistance actually received it.[27] That's because parents may not be aware of the assistance that is available to them, and even if they are, there is not always the supply of childcare centers or workers to meet the demand.

For example, a mother named Rhiannon Broschat was fired from her job at Whole Foods in 2014 for missing work when there was an unexpected school closure. She could not find backup care for her son, who could not be left alone. "If I could have found adequate childcare, I would have made it to work. I need my money. They try to play it like I was lazy," Broschat told *The Nation*.[28]

MAKING IMPOSSIBLE COMPROMISES

Though the majority of contemporary mothers work for pay, what stuck out in my interviews with several of them was that they felt isolated in their attempts to manage their jobs and care for their children. Each felt like they had to forge an individualized path of support, and many were shocked at how difficult it proved to be. If they had partners, they all felt that their children's care ultimately fell on their shoulders. No matter how privileged these women were, it was surprising to them how little agency they felt they ultimately had.

When Christine Hernandez, thirty-seven, had her first child, she had just started a job as an education director at a nonprofit. Meanwhile, she had a second, part-time contract job that she did on weekends and at night. "I was probably working fifty to sixty hours every week," she said. Despite her long hours, she did not realize she might not be eligible for even unpaid leave from her full-time job through the Family and Medical Leave Act, which stipulates that you must work for a company for twelve months to qualify.[29] The company did end up giving her a period of unpaid leave, but she had to fight for it. She ended up resigning while still on leave and keeping the contract gig, which was fully remote and allowed her to manage work and caregiving. Christine's husband is an accountant and made more money than she did, even though she has a master's degree.

While Christine was happy to work part time remotely around her son's schedule, she felt judged by the moms around her in New York City, most of whom worked full time outside the home. They would make little comments about how stay-at-home moms had "all the time in the world," which made her feel "not as cool, not as liberal and modern," she said.

Her son was two and a half when Christine got pregnant with her second child, and by that time her family was living in Long Island. Her contract job had offered her additional hours and "to take the lead on this project they were doing. It just so happened it would be beginning right around my due date," she said. "I could really use the extra hours—it was my only income. I felt I couldn't say no to it, so I said yes." She just didn't tell her boss she was pregnant.

This was an active choice, and a searing indictment of the American system of work. "Not only am I a temp employee and could be let go at any minute, but what if they say they can't fire me because I'm pregnant? Maybe they'll just pick someone else to do the project," she said. She was not entitled to leave of any sort, and she was afraid they'd force her to take unpaid time off "to heal," which she did not want to do.

She managed to keep the birth a secret—she told her employer she had a family emergency that day—and kept working. "I would set my older son up on the couch and put my baby in the carrier and rock him to sleep so they wouldn't hear a baby in the background" on work calls, she said.

Things only got weird when the pandemic began, Christine said, because her boss started sharing more about her personal life— about the ambulances rushing by and how hard it was to homeschool her daughter. Christine would talk about her son, but began to feel guilty about her additional "secret baby." Then she was angry that she felt guilty because she didn't think a man would be shamed into sharing personal information with his boss. "I feel guilty because I'm not being vulnerable with my supervisor? Why should I care about that aspect of it, it has nothing to do with my work," she said.

Her guilt certainly dissipated when she was laid off after the big project wrapped. Now she has a full-time job, with benefits. She still works remotely and keeps her younger son home with her because the cost of day care would take up most of her salary. She and her husband are talking about moving to a less costly area and having him stay home while she becomes the breadwinner for a while.

Mothers are trained to feel like they should be grateful for whatever they get, Christine said, for having a healthy baby, for having any job at all. "I guess the moral of the story is I learned to ask for what I deserve," she said.[30]

Dreama James, forty-three, who is a fast-food worker in Georgia and a mom of five, was able to manage her caretaking responsibilities fairly well for a long time. She has also been a home health-care aide in the past, and she said she worked when her children, who are now twenty-three, twenty-two, twenty-one, eighteen, and thirteen, were in school. In a pinch, she was usually able to bring them with her. "I had to work, their father wasn't very good about keeping a job, and he also wasn't able to watch them." It was going decently well, she said, "until corona hit."

Dreama was deemed an "essential worker," and her youngest, Conner, who was eleven at the time, was too old to be in day care, but too young to stay home alone for long periods of time. At first, her job would not allow her to bring him with her. She took twelve weeks of paid leave through the Families First Coronavirus Response Act in the spring of 2020, which allowed her to stay home and get two-thirds of her pay (the FFCRA expired at the end of 2020).[31] That 66 percent of her salary was not enough for her family to stay afloat, and Dreama had to make hard choices about her family's needs. She went into debt. "That's where credit cards come in," she said.

When Conner had to go back to virtual school in the fall, Dreama was trapped. She was out of leave, and she could not afford the $280 a week it would cost for a tutor to help her son. Her manager would not allow Conner to do virtual school from the restaurant's lobby; he said he wasn't running a day care. She found a friend who would watch her son, but Dreama still had to cut back on hours to monitor her son's learning and deal with school closures.

Ultimately, Dreama's manager was having so much trouble finding reliable employees that he started letting her bring Conner to work with her. "It still wasn't the best situation," she said. "He's sitting in [the fast-food restaurant] with a computer and I'm not sure if he's doing his schoolwork or not, and we had to go all over the same stuff again."

She also felt like her work was not taking the proper precautions to protect her family's health. "We had four separate incidents where people had corona. We weren't even told by the upper management, we were told by the people who had it," she said. "The worst was I was in the drive-thru window one day and a lady sneezed on me. I got so sick, I thought I was going to die." It turned out it was the flu, not COVID-19. But coronavirus "was a constant worry. I was going to work and I could possibly bring that home to my kids."

When we spoke in July 2021, Dreama said Conner was spending the summer with his dad. But she's worried about what's going to happen in the fall. Georgia had lifted its mask mandate, and when I first spoke to her, her son was too young for the vaccine. "With so many variants coming out, you can't know how to protect them," she said. She's still working her way out of the debt she accrued while staying home with her son. "I think the medical leave shouldn't have been just twelve weeks," Dreama said. "When your school shuts down because of a health emergency, you can't just rely on anyone to watch your child."[32]

Patrice Gamble, twenty-seven, who lives in New Jersey, is also struggling to get the childcare she had in place before the pandemic. Her son, who is two, had been attending a corporate-sponsored day care, which Patrice accessed through her mother's workplace. That day care has been closed since March 2020, and when I spoke to her in June 2021, she didn't know when it would reopen. Even at the reduced rate, her son's day care is expensive. "I pay pretty much my rent in day care, that's what it was costing me, that's with a sponsored day care that gave me a discount," she said.

Patrice works in public relations, and her partner is a tow-truck driver. He is considered an essential worker and so she has been home with their child without much help. She relies on family members, but even so, "My days are much longer than people think they are. I get up around five or six, so I can get up before my kid. Frequently, I close my laptop at six but then at nine, I'm signing back on. There's many days where I go to bed at midnight and wake up at five a.m.," Patrice said.

Still, her current job is much better than her previous one, where she felt she was treated as less capable after she became a parent. "I was excited to get back to work," Patrice said. "But I was kind of treated as if I was now incompetent. They gave me very light work, and it remained that way for months. I asked for more work, and they would say, 'Here's something easy for you to do,'" she said.[33]

THEY'RE TAKING CARE OF YOUR HEALTH, BUT NO ONE IS TAKING CARE OF THEIRS

I spoke to several higher-income mothers, many of whom have inflexible working hours and not much support for their caretaking responsibilities. But the most glaring lack of support was ironically for women who work as doctors and dentists; they're taking care of our health, but their employers are not looking out for theirs.

A woman I'll call Heather, thirty-nine, who is a maternal-fetal medicine specialist and mom of three, said that when she was pregnant with her second child, she was starting her first attending physician faculty position at a big public university, and had just finished a fellowship in high-risk pregnancies. She was thirty-two weeks pregnant when she began her new role, and she didn't realize until she was in her orientation that the university doesn't guarantee paid leave. She pulled the benefits person aside and asked what her options were.

In short: Heather had nothing. She hadn't accrued any paid time off in the form of sick days or vacation because she just started the job. Her health insurance from the university wouldn't kick in immediately. "I essentially panicked. How can I be an ob-gyn physician, a pregnancy specialist, having a baby with no protection? No leave, no insurance, no anything," Heather said.

Luckily Heather did not go into preterm labor, so her insurance kicked in before the birth of her child, and the cost of the birth would not have to be paid out of pocket. And also luckily, Heather's supervisor was sympathetic. They said they disagreed with the university's policy and asked her how much time she needed. She asked for twelve weeks, and her boss told her she would be technically working from home during that period, so she could continue to get paid and keep her job, but she wouldn't really have to do very much. Her boss told her, If you get emails, try to answer them periodically.

Heather said that she had another faculty member urging her to start a petition to change the university's policy, but she hesitated because she didn't want to get her boss in trouble. She was also brand new to the role; she didn't want to get a reputation as a difficult person. She has many supportive colleagues who are also mothers of small children, and she said some of them pushed themselves to return to work just a month after giving birth because they felt such a sense of obligation to their jobs and their patients.

She said she struggles with guilt over choosing to be an academic researcher. "This is something I think about all the time," Heather said. "I could choose a different career path and have a better family life. It's tough because in contrast with my own mother, who had to work two jobs as a single mom, I am actively choosing to work more for my own professional fulfillment, and that adds its own layer of mom guilt."[34]

Alexandra Hochster, thirty-nine, who has a five-year-old and a baby in Philadelphia, said that when she became a dentist, she was told it was a great career for mothers. "It's so flexible, you can make your own schedule," they said. "And that's really not what I have seen." The reality is that it's a patient-facing job. "If you've arranged your schedule to see the dentist, no one wants to hear the dentist can't be there because her kid is throwing up at school. But what am I supposed to do if my kid is throwing up at school?"

Her husband is a lawyer and does his fair share, she said, and his job has a bit more flexibility than hers. But Alexandra did not get any paid leave for either of her pregnancies because she only gets paid based on the procedures she does and how much the insurance companies reimburse her practice—she's not on salary. She's an associate in a small practice, which she does not own. "There's no HR in dentistry," she said.

Furthermore, her taking weeks of leave causes a chain reaction in the practice. "It's not just about the financials," though certainly her family can't afford for her to take a very long leave. It's also, "The other dentist is doing the job by themselves. My patients are getting seen by me or not getting seen at all. It puts a burden on everybody else," she said.

Typically she is the only dentist who works on Fridays, and the hygienist and the receptionist don't work on Fridays, so when she's on leave, they have to shift their hours. "You're at the top of the food chain so that's on you, and I don't feel good screwing up everybody's work schedule." As a result, she is taking just six weeks of leave with her new baby.[35]

PAID LEAVE AND
"RADICAL FLEXIBILITY"

Because I also worked for a small company, I had to schedule my two months of maternity leave far in advance. It made sense because my temporary replacement had to know her start date, and I didn't want to leave anyone in the lurch. My second daughter was due on July 8, and so I started my leave over the July Fourth holiday and was scheduled to return the day after Labor Day.

July 8 rolled around and I was nowhere near labor. As the days of my leave ticked by, I started getting increasingly anxious, knowing that I was waddling around in 90-degree heat, pissing away my maternity leave without an actual baby to care for. I tried to make myself useful. I rearranged the furniture in the baby's room, which was a makeshift third bedroom we fashioned from part of the living room, using a curtain to cordon off the area. I cooked elaborate dinners and made them Pinterest pretty, arranging the vegetables in a cold noodle salad in a rainbow of red cabbage, carrots, yellow peppers, and bean sprouts.

I also picked fights with my husband and begged my obstetrician to schedule me for an induction. He told me the practice wouldn't induce until forty-one weeks, and he put me on the morning schedule for forty-one weeks and one day. In the afternoon on the day before my induction, I started bleeding lightly and feeling the early rumblings of real contractions, none of that Braxton-Hicks fake nonsense.

My second birth was so different from my first. I got to the hospital around 6:00 p.m. and was admitted quickly. I got my epidural right away. I watched an episode of *Keeping Up with the Kardashians* in total comfort, and when the nurse came in to check me, she said, "Wow, you're ready to go." The obstetrician came in, I pushed three times, and my second, perfect daughter flew out of me. At 8 pounds, 6 ounces, another generously sized baby though not quite as enormous as her older sister.

My second maternity leave was also quite different. I didn't need to make mom friends—by this time many of my actual friends had babies, and I had made solid and organic-feeling connections with those preschool moms. I was blessed with another pretty easy baby, and she slept just enough that I didn't feel too crazy.

It might seem obvious to point out, but the main reason that my second leave felt so relaxed is because it was paid. Instead of being worried about my entire career disappearing, I knew I had a job to go back to, one that allowed me to take a true break. I didn't check my work email at all until a week before my return, and because my work environment was generally casual and accepting, I decided to put up this out-of-office auto reply:

> I will automatically delete all emails sent to this address while I am away, so if it's something terribly urgent or time-sensitive (as in, you are on fire and I am the only person in the contiguous United States who can put it out OR you want to give me money but only in August), you can reach me at my Gmail account.
>
> Otherwise, please reach back out in September!

Some length of paid leave for caretaking should be a basic right for all workers, not just parents. Almost every single person will have to take care of someone else at some point in their many decades of paid work, and no one should have to worry about potentially losing a job on top of that. It's the very least that can be done to treat American workers as fully human, with lives and connections outside of work.

The other part of what enabled me to manage my work and life is what McKinsey & Company calls "radical flexibility." What does that look like, in practice? Radical flexibility:

> goes beyond giving parents and other caregivers extra paid time off to take care of family needs. What if an employee needs every Tuesday afternoon off to care for a child or other family member? The response might be to give them a free floating day per week that they can take whenever they need it, no questions asked. Maybe some parents would love taking off from 3:00 p.m. until after dinner, then logging back in as needed after the kids are in bed.

The need for flexibility for parents has become even more clear since the beginning of the pandemic. In a December 2021 report, McKinsey noted that more parents than nonparents surveyed had left their jobs or were planning to, in large part because they needed that radical flexibility and weren't getting it from their current employers. They were more likely to take up gig work or start their own companies to get the flexibility they craved.[36]

Knowing that I had fairly radical flexibility in my job made me eager to go back to work in 2016. But of course, flexibility isn't everything. My eagerness dissipated considerably when the weekend before I was supposed to return, one of the company's founders threw herself into another social media disaster.

I knew that it wasn't my job to control her statements (and I found out the hard way I couldn't do it even if I tried), but every time she had another blunder it infuriated and hurt our readers, and it stressed and upset my team; they felt considerable blowback.

In retrospect it was the beginning of the end, and my experience, which had previously been mostly thrilling, though at times exasperating, just became painful. When my baby was a year and a half, I started looking seriously for a new job.

I had enough experience to know that I didn't want to leave one increasingly unhappy situation for another. So I only applied for jobs that I really wanted, at organizations I felt would provide me with greater financial stability—I really wanted a 401(k) again—and opportunities to be creative, and ideally to cover topics that meant something to readers. I did not plan on becoming a parent professionally, but that's what happened next.

FIVE

Social Media

"STOP WHINING AND COUNT YOUR BLESSINGS"

When I got the job to start a new parenting product, I felt like a career dream had been realized. Seven years after my disastrous work implosion, I had an extremely stable job: one that provided me with benefits, a 401(k) match, and a potential opportunity for advancement.

It was on that last front that I had a hint of concern. For a big chunk of my working life, I deliberately tried to make myself a generalist, even though my greatest interests were in what was considered women's media. I wrote about grizzly bear attacks and culture and politics because it was common knowledge in journalism circles that if you are considered solely a lady magazine person, you would not be taken seriously by hiring managers outside the so-called pink ghetto. Part of the reason I had taken that culture editor job that turned out to be a barf-covered disaster was because I had been working at a women's website and I didn't want to be pigeonholed forever.

Never mind the fact that I felt extremely passionate about all the topics that were cordoned off as "women's issues," or that I knew in my soul that topics like paid leave, childcare support, education, and abortion should be everybody's issues. The marginalization of topics like parenting in larger media organizations is just a microcosm of what happens in American society. Whenever something gets associated with women, no matter how vital it is to the world, it is seen as frivolous and nonessential.

The best part of my new job was that I thought I could actually change some things for the better, and make life a little easier for at least a few moms. My older daughter was five and my little one was two when I was hired at the *Times*. As a consumer of online parenting content, I knew exactly what was wrong with the articles I was reading and the images I was seeing, and I knew what I wanted to see change. The biggest problem I saw was the biased judgment in the framing of information that shouldn't be morally charged.

When my older daughter was a baby, I remember looking for advice on how to wean her. I recalled that every article and message board I found discussing weaning was aggressively pro–extended breastfeeding, and basically said, "If you must wean your baby on your own timetable, YOU MONSTER, I guess here's some cold cabbage leaves to stick in your bra."

It didn't matter to these random commenters that the scientific evidence for frozen cabbage leaves over other cold compresses was pretty weak,[1] or that they made me smell like rancid coleslaw. That was another major issue: much of the information—and there is just so, so much parenting information on the internet—was not evidence-based, even though many of the sources that were pushing antiscience information, especially about vaccines, mimicked the language of "research" and "studies" to seem like they were giving you medically vetted information.

Because there is just an avalanche of information about every parenting topic, even the most educated, informed parents struggle to sift through the data. Though in many ways modern American parenting is easier than it used to be (we have antibiotics, motor vehicles, and indoor plumbing), it is uniquely difficult in the amount of information we get about what we're supposed to be doing, and how high the stakes are made to seem about every minor decision.

The amount of drama I have witnessed over feeding children milk is a prime example of the inappropriately heightened stakes of every parental choice. Parents—and let's be honest, it's mothers—first wonder when they should introduce whole milk to their kids, or if they should introduce any kind of dairy at all, or stick to plant-based milks. Isn't dairy destroying the environment? If you're feeding milk at all, should it be organic? Will the antibiotics used in nonorganic milks cause early puberty? Does "natural" mean something different from "organic"? And do the cows need to be grass fed?

Then, if they have introduced milk into their children's diets, the next drama is over whether they should switch at some point from whole milk to 2 percent, 1 percent, or skim. The wrong choice at the wrong time could mean confining your child to a life of obesity and/or allergies. There is no sense of scale or context on the internet, and the passion total strangers have about feeding children the "correct" milk can feel as intense as their passion about climate change or cancer, especially when you're a vulnerable new parent just trying to do your best.

Recent studies have shown that somewhere between 75 and 98 percent of parents now look for health information online, and research suggests that for some subset of parents, online information seeking is associated with higher levels of anxiety, distress, and worry.[2] As the years go by, more and more parents get health information from social media, and that information may be even less verified and less reliable than the information that rises to the top on a Google search. To wit, anti-vaccine and anti-mask information spread like wildfire on social media during the pandemic, and some of the major superspreaders of health misinformation were moms.

The other big problem I saw online was the lack of diversity in the most popular parenting icons. I mean diversity in every possible sense of the word: The majority of them appeared to be white, thin, Christian, and wealthy. Although I know there are millions of moms Instagramming and TikTokking who do not fit these specific parameters, and *Parents* magazine recently launched a new digital magazine called *Kindred for Black Moms and Dads*,[3] the algorithm keeps serving me the toothy blondes, and every list of the top mom-fluencers is filled with these women.[4] Even though I try not to follow any of them, they haunt my "for you" and "discover" pages, dancing in their cavernous living rooms, posing in matching outfits with their "mini mes" and "littles."

These mothers always seem to be happy with their children— and they always have at least three of them. Whenever they refer to mental health or parenting difficulties, those problems are in the past. Their postpartum depression, or a family death, or their child's difficulty at school have been solved, juxtaposed with a beautiful image of open hands or a serene lake.

The influencers with hundreds of thousands or even millions of followers and who show up most frequently in my algorithm usually have a domestic or classically feminine inclination beyond motherhood, whether it's beauty (like Amber Fillerup Clark), clothing and decor (like Rach Parcell, formerly known as Pink Peonies), DIY renovation (Naomi Davis, aka Taza), or farming and cooking (like Hannah Neeleman of Ballerina Farm, an ex–ballet dancer, beauty queen, and mom of seven).

Sometimes they combine knowledge or education in the parenting space with perfectly curated imagery. As a mom who had her first baby during the pandemic explained to me over Twitter DM, "I think the internet thing that I've spent the most time thinking about is the influencers who are not just lifestyle, but use their lifestyles to try to promote their 'expertise.'" Like the Speech Sisters (a pair of blond baby and toddler sleep experts), Solid Starts (a mom who promotes "baby led weaning," an infant feeding method that purports to have all manner of benefits for children, but studies have shown is no better or worse than spoon-feeding),[5] and Taking Cara Babies (a controversial pediatric sleep expert).

"I've spent so much time scrolling through Instagram late at night and it's just weird, like, am I supposed to trust them because they're ~aspirationally pretty~ or because they sell a $99 course to fix my problems? Are these even problems?" the new mom wonders.

Even when these online moms are playing at relatability, the #perfectlyimperfect moms, as the online motherhood researcher Kathryn Jezer-Morton calls them,[6] are actually hewing incredibly close to the old-fashioned ideals. "Most images that are tagged with #perfectlyimperfect or #motherhoodunplugged represent conventionally "perfect" women—attractive, carefully groomed, usually white, posing for selfies that reinforce many of the same old beauty and femininity norms that have dogged women since the dawn of time. Online motherhood has always contained its share of disingenuousness disguised as relatability, and this is the latest version," Jezer-Morton wrote.

I wanted to create a site that was evidence-based, as unbiased as possible, and that allowed for parents to tell stories that were truly imperfect, where they wrestled with the hard and sometimes ugly parts of being a parent. I wanted to talk about the joys, too, but not in a saccharine, smarmy way. I always felt infantilized reading that "hey mama!" tone, like these outlets talked to me as if I'd had a lobotomy, not a baby.

And what the evidence on most topics shows is that there isn't one way to be a good parent; there are many, many ways. Most things are shades of gray, and largely dictated by culture and the individual personalities and circumstances in your home. I wanted to show that nuance whenever possible. I never wanted parents to feel bad about themselves after reading something I had written or edited; I wanted them to feel capable and heard.

I didn't feel like I was reinventing the wheel. There have been many publications and individual writers over the years doing real scientific research, showing a diverse range of experiences and backgrounds, and telling the truth about motherhood more generally. In fact, a *New York Times* article about a new parenting magazine called *Children* almost a century ago reads like my mission statement.

The editors of *Children*, which launched in 1926, relied on expert-backed advice and eschewed the soppy tone, which was rampant even then. According to the *Times*: "So much sentimental slush has been talked and written about the 'defenseless young' that an involuntary fear steals over the reader who picks up a magazine dedicated to them. He need dread no sugary uplift in the tone of the newcomer. It starts off with frank and sprightly disregard of the convention which makes all babies little angels."[7] In 1929, *Children* was renamed *Parents*,[8] and that magazine still lives on today.

What made me different from the early editors of *Children* is I had the internet, and the biggest venue in modern journalism actually putting money behind a parenting product. I didn't want to waste the money or the moment.

In some ways, the internet has been incredible for allowing mothers to share their darkest and most conflicted thoughts. The popular website Scary Mommy has published countless anonymous submissions, like Confessional #27590: "If I could turn back time, I wouldn't have had a child, nor would I have married either H, though my current H is pretty okay. I just would have been happier single and living alone."

Obviously, the internet is also the reason I have a career writing about motherhood. And yet when women write about how mothers cannot live up to the unreasonable and often nonsensical ideals of our culture, they often get flack for even mildly threatening the status quo. I have written publicly about my prenatal depression twice in nine years, and both times I wrote about it, I got feedback from multiple readers about how people with mental illness shouldn't have children at all.

This is a typical comment: "Perhaps such women who have so many mental health issues, should not be having children at all. Many mental health issues have an inheritable component, and the stress of being a parent is going to put a fragile person at significant risk. I just can't imagine such a person can be a very successful parent to a child."[9]

Does this person think 20 percent of moms are truly unfit to parent? Because at least a fifth of women have either prenatal or postpartum depression, and there's no way to predict before you are pregnant whether you will get depressed. Some people believe if you're not "happy" all the time, you shouldn't be a mother.

The blowback got even more intense during the pandemic. Every time I wrote about how badly mothers were struggling both mentally and economically, I got feedback that said, basically, moms need to quit complaining. This is what they signed up for when they had kids.

"Parenthood has become a choice for men and women of every economic strata in America. If you are not prepared to parent, under any and all circumstances, do not procreate. Family, especially children, can be the greatest comfort in adversity (the [sic] is actually why people have them). Stop whining and count your blessings," said one absolute crank, who apparently is not aware that Roe v. Wade was being dismantled.[10]

Most of the time I dismiss these commenters as ignorant jerks, but in my darker moments they make me question myself: Am I really somehow constitutionally unfit to be a mother? It's in these mood pockets that I am vulnerable to those perfect, blond momfluencers and their gleaming bright lives. I see their photographs juxtaposed with their sunny captions and some small part of me believes that they are more naturally suited to being moms than I am.

Sometime in the summer of 2021, @amberfillerup posted herself in a white dress on top of a mountain with her three kids and her husband, all grinning ear to ear, with the caption "Life is so fun with them."[11] She posed with her littlest one in matching swimsuits, which she is also selling: "this floral makes me so happy!"[12]

I thought of my kids, who have had very definite opinions of what they wanted to wear since they could speak, and their choices were never Instagram perfect. Are the influencers' kids just better behaved? Or do they have a cattle prod behind the scenes? I know that they have problems like any parent, and that their two-year-old probably threw a tantrum either right before or right after the photo was taken. Still, I'm completely seduced, and shamed, by the image.

Theoretically, we could have created an entirely new paradigm for mothers when parenting moved online. We could have made room for all different kinds of family formations, for ambivalence and nuance, and we could have elevated high-quality research and presented it in an accessible way. Instead, we exalted the same old-fashioned ideals, and then weaponized them against mothers who don't conform.

"If you think about fashion, representation has really changed" in the past five years, Kathryn Jezer-Morton, who is also a doctoral candidate in sociology at Concordia University, told me. We see more body positivity, gender inclusivity, and racial diversity from the fashion and beauty industries now, and it feels like some fashion and beauty bloggers are creating a new paradigm. "But we haven't seen a change in the way that motherhood is represented. Everyone who is doing the real talk stuff is in conversation with the perfect." Which is to say, even the moms who are parodying and dismantling the beach-body blondes are acknowledging that uniform ideal as they are pointing out how oppressive it is.[13]

I don't mean that all of the mominternet (momternet?) is bad. For some women in conservative communities, the internet is the only way for them to have a public voice and has allowed them to earn money while also caring for their children. For other women, social media has given them practical tips that improve their day-to-day— any information that helps you install a cursed car seat is worth its weight in gold.

Some spaces online have saved women's lives, have provided solace and connection, and have offered a different vision of motherhood. But increasingly, the corners where the "real talk" is happening are private. Why would you want to open your most vulnerable self up to an unflinchingly cruel and contextless crowd?

To figure out how we got here, I talked to editors who worked on the earliest motherhood websites, scholars at the intersection of the internet and mom culture, and social media moms of today. The answer boils down to the monetization of motherhood in online spaces, and it has chilling effects on the rest of us.

THE CONFESSIONAL AGE

Online mom content was in its infancy in the mid-aughts, when the first wave of bloggers and websites about motherhood began to find their audience. At that point, motherhood chat was mostly confined to message boards on sites like UrbanBaby and BabyCenter. And lots of parents were flocking to the internet to tell their raw and unfiltered truth, and to find community. Jezer-Morton, the online researcher, calls this wave "the Confessional Age," and she estimates it was from 2001 to 2009.

Liz Gumbinner, who would ultimately top many lists of influential mom bloggers for her website Mom 101, said that she didn't even know what a blog really was in the early aughts. "I thought blogs were like Talking Points Memo," she said, referencing a political blog that launched in 2000. Gumbinner just wanted to be a columnist. "My goal was writing, not to be famous." She was working in advertising, and she thought her blog could be a showcase for her work.

Gumbinner launched her blog in 2006, and because she had a baby, her life was about "scary new mom things," she said—so that's what she wrote about. She wasn't trying to create an aspirational visual world, and she wasn't trying to attract advertisers. She didn't even know advertisers would be interested. The tagline of Mom 101 was "I don't know what I'm doing either."[14]

Denene Millner was a columnist at *Parenting* magazine (a different publication from *Parents* magazine) when she started My Brown Baby in 2008. She had previously been an editor at the magazine. "What I found working at *Parenting* magazine and then also as a columnist was that Black voices were generally ignored," she said. When she was an editor, she would ask questions like: Why aren't we talking to Black mothers? Showing their perspective? Why aren't we interviewing them? Why are the few Black children in our photographs so light skinned?

She said she was told: "I had to pretend the reader was a solidly middle-class to upper-class white woman in the Midwest. If we didn't funnel all the stories through that lens, it wasn't for *Parenting*."[15]

Things didn't improve much when she got her column; she felt she still had to write for an audience that was perceived to be white and middle to upper class. "All these mommy blogs were starting to form. I was writing this column that required I be me but not me, and be authentic but not too authentic. So I just decided I would start my own blog." Before she was a parenting writer and editor, Millner had been a political journalist and an entertainment journalist, and she approached her blogging from a newsy point of view. Her first blog post was about Bristol Palin's pregnancy; she pointed out the hypocrisy of commentators who claimed it was not a news story. Millner knew that if Sasha or Malia Obama had turned up pregnant at sixteen, the response "would have been a referendum on Black motherhood."

Readers appreciated that Millner "dug deep into this neurosis that this country has when it comes to Black motherhood and everybody else," she said. She realized: "I don't have to talk to this one particular audience that I don't know or care about—I can write about my real experiences and the experiences of my friends." Although there were other Black mom bloggers out there, Millner was one of the few who was writing specifically for a Black audience. "It became this huge, huge deal," she said.[16]

When the website Babble.com launched in 2006, it had goals so similar to mine when I launched NYT Parenting that reading its original press release made me laugh because it confirms something I always tell my writers: There's nothing new under the sun. Babble was originally an offshoot of the then-popular and now-defunct website Nerve, which was dedicated to quality writing about sex and relationships, and according to its original mission statement, written by editor-in-chief Ada Calhoun:

> Babble will be a revolution in parenting magazines: a publication that talks to parents like fun, smart, intellectually curious people. It will apply Nerve's tradition of irreverent honesty about sex to the experience of parenting without the infantilizing, hyper-judgmental tone, and acquisitive baby-as-accessory bent of so much of today's parenting fare.

Gwynne Watkins, who was an editor at Babble from 2006 to 2010, said that when the site first launched, "We got a lot of positive feedback. A lot of parents were coming out of the woodwork wanting to write for us, and said they had been waiting for a smart publication around parenting . . . We got a lot of non-parents reading, too, who were curious about the experience of being a parent. I felt we were really hitting this universal thing. They want honesty, they want to know the weird stuff."

One of Babble's most popular columns was called "Bad Parent," and it had a huge following, Watkins said. "It ran the gamut from parents admitting they had a favorite kid, or that they were worried their kid wasn't smart, to retellings of disastrous outings."[17] This column debuted before Ayelet Waldman, the essayist and novelist, published her collection of essays called *Bad Mother*, in 2009, which pivoted off a highly controversial and viral 2005 "Modern Love" column in the *New York Times*. In this column Waldman declared, "If a good mother is one who loves her child more than anyone else in the world, I am not a good mother. I am in fact a bad mother. I love my husband more than I love my children."[18]

At the same time as these grittier depictions of motherhood were gaining press attention and readers, another group of motherhood bloggers began depicting a very different and much cheerier vision of parenthood. They were young, beautiful, fashionable, and they made motherhood seem effortless—the aforementioned Naomi Davis, whose blog was then called Rockstar Diaries, was among that group, which included Stephanie Nielson of the NieNie Dialogues and Natalie Holbrook, then known as Nat the Fat Rat. These women were also all Mormon.

Emily Matchar, author of *Homeward Bound: Why Women Are Embracing the New Domesticity*, described the secular appeal of the Mormon set in a 2011 article in Salon. At the time, Matchar didn't have kids, though she is now the mother of two. Matchar had no illusions about what Mormon living was like behind the scenes because she was married to a former Latter-Day Saint. She knew she did not want to live that life. And yet:

> To use a word that makes me cringe, these blogs are weirdly "up-lifting." To read Mormon lifestyle blogs is to peer into a strange and fascinating world where the most fraught issues of modern living—marriage and child rearing—appear completely unproblematic. This seems practically subversive to someone like me, weaned on an endless media parade of fretful stories about "work-life balance" and soaring divorce rates and the perils of marrying too young/too old/too whatever. And don't even get me started on the Mommy Blogs, which make parenthood seem like a vale of judgment and anxiety, full of words like "guilt" and "chaos" and "BPA-free" and "episiotomy." Read enough of these, and you'll be ready to remove your own ovaries with a butter knife.[19]

Theoretically, there was enough room on the big internet for these worlds to coexist: the sometimes unpleasant real talk that scares the shit out of childless lurkers but that offers solace and visibility to the moms struggling through it; the political commentary and nuanced vision of Black motherhood; and the gilded palace of momfluencers that presents a spotless and pleasant world for anyone to dip into and out of, even as we know in our hearts it's not the full story.

But when advertisers realized what a gold mine the mamasphere was, who do you think they wanted to put more money behind: self-proclaimed "bad moms" who admitted things like, "I am the only woman in Mommy and Me who seems to be, well, getting any,"[20] or moms who "focus more on the lovely and the beautiful," as the Mormon blogger Natalie Holbrook did?[21]

Unsurprisingly, the lovely and the beautiful sold more onesies than the cranky and tired. Though some of the cranky and tired, like

Heather Armstrong of Dooce.com, did incredibly well for themselves for a while there in 2008 and 2012, before Instagram became ascendant. It's also worth noting that for all her crankiness, Armstrong is still white, model tall and thin, blond, and formerly Mormon.

Creating quality content is a full-time job, one that frankly *deserves to* be paid for. Blogging or Instagramming from home is also a way for moms who lack structural support or a desire to work outside the home to earn an income while also caring for their children, and that's a good thing.

Still, according to news reports from that period, almost no one in the online motherhood market was striking it rich. "The best estimates are that perhaps only a few dozen women are making big bucks blogging, from their sponsorships and advertising deals on their sites, speaking engagements and other media gigs related to the brands they have built with their blogs," an *ABC News* report from 2011 noted.[22]

Watkins said that at Babble, when Fortune 500 companies came knocking, "the publisher started pulling content that the advertisers didn't like, including some of the big buzzy pieces we had launched with. And the website very quickly became geared more toward pleasing advertisers than creating something new," she said. "Advertisers wanted our young, hip audience; they didn't want anything that could potentially be controversial or brand damaging."[23]

They also weren't very interested in non-white moms. Denene Millner said that she was making money off sponsored posts on My Brown Baby, but only while she was still also a columnist at *Parenting*. "I promise you, the second I no longer wrote the column, the amount of money people were throwing at me eventually dried up," she said.

And anytime she wrote about race for *Parenting*, or spoke about her blog on TV, she received the most vile, racist emails in her inbox. "It left me open and vulnerable to the crazy," as she put it. When she was on *Today*, arguably the biggest venue for America's mothers at the time, "I never realized any kind of contracts from that. I never realized any kind of monetary value. I never realized a bump in traffic or audience." All she got was "an avalanche of racist comments."[24]

Ultimately, Disney purchased Babble in 2011 for a reported $40 million.[25] According to Watkins, in the intervening years, Babble was stripped of all of its edge and quality, becoming a content mine. In its first year after acquisition, Babble released a list of its top one hundred most influential mom bloggers. Every single mother in Babble's top ten that year was white, with Black moms like Denene and Kelly Wickham of Mocha Momma much farther down the list.[26]

Babble was eventually shuttered "quietly" in 2019.[27] Liz Gumbinner, who still runs Mom 101 in addition to working part time, launched a business in 2006 called Cool Mom Picks, which focuses on discovering and sharing products and tech for parents. While Cool Mom Picks does make some money from advertising (as Gumbinner aptly puts it, "We deserve to make a living"), "our heart is always about supporting moms," and they have always put small, mom-run businesses first, she says.

Millner said she stopped blogging at My Brown Baby because she got tired. She was writing five days a week, and after Trayvon Martin's death in 2012, "It eventually felt like the only thing I was writing about was Black trauma and pain and that's not why I started the blog. At the same time while I'm walking through this fire every night, people weren't really reading it." Bigger venues had started to pay attention to the issues Millner had been raising on her blog, and people's attention spans were already flagging from the onslaught of social media. "People just stopped wanting to read a thousand words" when they could read a hundred words on Twitter, she said.[28]

At the beginning of the 2010s, everything began to shift away from individual blogs and websites, and toward social media. For moms in particular, YouTube and Instagram became the primary venues for their content. And as mom bloggers and advertisers pivoted to social and video, their businesses became even less about words, and more about the images they could project. And the business of online motherhood went from "a few dozen" moms eking out a living to a multibillion-dollar industry,[29] selling products to a market of millennial moms that has over $2 trillion to spend.[30]

ENTER THE BLOGGERNACLE

Many observers of mom influencers have noticed that the successful ones are disproportionately members of the Church of Jesus Christ of Latter-Day Saints. There are only 6.7 million Mormons in the United States; they make up about 2 percent of the population.[31] And yet as the author and journalist Jo Piazza points out in her highly entertaining podcast, *Under the Influence*, there are so many prominent Mormon mom influencers that they have a nickname: "the Bloggernacle."[32]

There are a number of deeply rooted theological and historical reasons why Mormons disproportionately own the influencer market. One, as Piazza points out, is that record keeping is considered a "sacred duty."[33] Recording history was a tenet passed down to Joseph Smith, the founder of Mormonism, by the Lord. According to the official church historian and recorder, Elder Steven E. Snow, the Lord "taught Joseph Smith and other early leaders that 'there shall be a record kept among you,' that the records and histories should be kept 'continually,' and that doing so would 'be for the good of the church, and for the rising generations.'"[34]

A differentiator of Mormonism from other Christian sects is that they view their canon of scripture as open, and emphasize the fact that God can give revelations directly to man. So keeping track of revelations is an important part of their theology—but it also means that Mormon mothers were proto-blogging about their families before blogs existed.[35] Moving that work onto the internet was a fairly seamless process.

Another key part of Mormon teachings is to emphasize the positive, or "focus more on the lovely and the beautiful," as Natalie Holbrook put it to Emily Matchar in 2011. According to Mormon historian Kristine Haglund, one of Mormonism's 13 Articles of Faith, which are the "basic points of belief of The Church of Jesus Christ of Latter-Day Saints,"[36] is seized upon by many mom influencers to give a religious dimension to their work. The particular line from the Articles of Faith that is oft-cited in pursuit of "aesthetic ideals" online is: "If there is anything virtuous, lovely, or of good report or praiseworthy, we seek after these things."[37]

Mormon values also include a health code, said Caroline Kline, assistant director for global Mormon studies at Claremont Graduate University, and they are not supposed to drink coffee or alcohol. "There is this idea that the body is sacred, and to take care of the body is a sacred responsibility," Kline said. So pragmatic ideals of physical beauty, both of the self and of the home, "can have a spiritual overlay."[38]

Perhaps most importantly, Mormonism tells women that their highest spiritual calling is as mothers. According to Kline, "Several decades ago, the First Presidency of the Church stated, 'Motherhood is near to divinity. It is the highest, holiest service to be assumed by mankind. It places her who honors its holy calling and service next to the angels.'"[39]

Mormon feminists critique this equivalence. As Kline points out, "Many Mormon feminists—with and without children—are fundamentally uncomfortable with having their identity as human beings reduced to this one maternal concept."[40] But it is still the gendered norm that is embraced by the church hierarchy.

Furthermore, "It is a Mormon imperative to share the gospel with other people, and it's not just something a missionary is supposed to do," Kline said. Mormon women are also encouraged to be educated, Kline said, and these highly educated and capable women may feel that they should "perform some form of religious commitment to gender roles and domesticity" because they have been told how holy motherhood is.[41] And so by showing the world their domestic idyll, putting motherhood first, seeking out pretty things, they are not only finding a voice for themselves and their values, but are subtly prose-lytizing to us all.

Meg Conley, who is now thirty-six, was a twentysomething new mom in Utah when she started posting to Instagram. Because she was raised Mormon, she said she had been told her whole life that being a homemaker was "not just what you should do, but a divine calling." She wanted to be a writer since she had held a book, and had been encouraged to go to college, but dropped out of Utah State University when she got married at twenty-one because "that's what Mormons do." "My church culture sort of overwhelmed my home culture," as her parents told her that she was here to "become," and she could become anything she wanted to—and that could include motherhood, but it wasn't the "ultimate measure of becoming."

Meg had her first baby, a girl, at twenty-four, and then experi-enced postpartum depression, which her obstetrician did not take particularly seriously. "I said, I don't want to kill myself but I don't want to live, and what he hears is 'I don't want to kill myself,'" she said. Meg stared at walls for six months before she could literally and metaphorically start looking out windows. "I loved her, and I loved my husband but I could not figure out how to be happy making a home," she said. "I started understanding that homemaking might be a concept. But hospital corners on a bed, at least for me, is not homemaking. If that's not homemaking, what am I going to do?"[42]

For Meg, posting to Instagram, which she began doing in 2012, when she had her second child, helped her find a community, and a voice. As she put it in her newsletter, *Home Culture*:

Much of my time was spent alone with my kids. I felt both overwhelmed and underwhelmed by the work of the day. With Instagram, I made a chain of meaning out of the pictures I posted for my couple of dozen followers. A baby on her blanket on the ground. A pile of dirty dishes. This new thing called a "selfie." It was my turn to sit at the park, checking for Instagram posts from women writing about being alone in their houses with their kids too. Their confessional rants about dirty dishes and housework felt like communion. As the platform gained popularity, that communion became community.

The women put up pictures of their dirty kitchens, their crying children. They shared stories about birth and house work. Some of these women had jobs outside of the home, but many did not. But I knew they were working, even if they weren't paid for their work. They were doing the work I did. Instagram helped make carework visible and, for some moms, it made carework profitable.[43]

Kathryn Jezer-Morton calls this period, from roughly 2009 to 2015, the "Early Sponcon Age." "Sponcon" stands for "sponsored content," and it was when brands began to realize they needed more than display ads to get people to buy their products; they needed direct testimony from moms. That's when the paeans to particular baby wraps began, but before #ads proliferated.

Farah Miller, my colleague at the *Times* who launched the *Huffington Post's* parenting vertical in 2011 and then went to work at Facebook and Instagram in 2016, had a front-row seat to the evolution of momfluencing. "It mimicked the rest of the internet in a lot of ways," she said. "Blogs were funny and more fun, and then everything sort of shifted, to be more about social and more about Instagram. If you put it on Instagram, it had to look a certain way in order to do well."[44] Miller believes the emphasis on the good and the pretty was somewhat built into Instagram's DNA—for a long time the only measurement of success was to "like" something.

Part of the shift from blogs to visuals also made parenting media less about the parents and what they might be going through, and more about the kids and the lifestyle. "When you had to focus on pictures, they became about your kids or your house. Even if you were going to write something really heartfelt, you had to have something perfect to show with it," Miller said.[45]

In the mid-teens, brands were throwing influencer-friendly parties constantly, tossing out cheese sticks like confetti. Meg Conley would occasionally be invited to these parties in Utah, and she described them like this: "A brand is releasing a new juice box. They'd send a hundred cases of this juice box to the mini-influencer who is going to have a party centered around them, and have a photoshoot, and seventy-five women in the community would attend."

"I think in my little corner of Mormon women, what you saw was lots of them leaping into the platform like it was going to save their damn lives, because they were isolated and ambitious and creative, and this was a way to figure out how to solve for all those things," Conley said. "For some of them it did." For her it did not. Although she presented the then-popular "flat lay" of products, arranged just so for sponsorship because her family needed the money, "I was seeking meaning in my work, and that left me feeling empty, because I didn't want my work to be a performance."[46]

The extent to which what we see is a performance was underlined by a 2019 *Elle* magazine profile of Natalie Holbrook. Natalie is the Mormon mom influencer who had previously topped many lists of the most influential moms online as Nat the Fat Rat and then Hey Natalie Jean. (She changed her blog's name to something blander and more palatable to advertisers at the request of her management agency.) The profile, by Nona Willis Aronowitz, outlines the way Natalie's life was falling apart behind the scenes as she was selling the picture-perfect image of her chubby toddler and her handsome husband: "I had to reckon with the fact that I'd been lying to people,"

Natalie (who now uses her maiden name, Lovin) tells me now. "I had to go back on my word and say 'Just kidding, I was actually miserable, I just didn't tell you.'" All those years curating and cropping her life, she says, "I was erasing evidence. I was erasing myself."[47]

As Natalie was trying to pull herself back together after separating from her husband and shuttering her blog, she read *The Feminine Mystique*. Just like the white, educated housewives in the 1960s, "when she read Friedan, she realized she'd been putting up with men's crap her whole life," and decided not to reconcile with her now ex.

THE EXHIBITOR ECONOMY

In her podcast *Under the Influence*, Jo Piazza outlines the basic economics of what she calls "the mom influencing industrial complex."

> There are plenty of aspiring influencers who lose money. They lose more money trying to be an influencer than they bring in. On the flip side of that, plenty of women have found themselves in the very comfortable position of making between $50,000 and $75,000 a year by monetizing their Instagrams. That is more than the average teacher's salary. Some women even make so much money that their husbands are quitting their own jobs to manage their wives' Instagram brands.

These very lucky few, with over five hundred thousand Instagram followers, can make millions, Piazza explains. The typical payment formula is simple: They make $100 per ten thousand followers on a post sponsored by a brand. So if you have a million followers, you can make $10,000 on a single sponsored post. According to Influencer Marketing Hub, a research agency that covers the influencer market, to make the median US income of $34,000 a year as a You-Tube influencer, you need about thirteen million yearly views—a level of success very few people achieve.[48]

To make enough money to be the equivalent of a decently paid full-time job, you need to have at least a hundred and fifty thousand followers, with a high engagement rate, Piazza told me; you can't just buy followers and fake it, you need to have real fans. And the time spent cultivating your audience and lining up sponsorships is considerable. Piazza estimates that these women are working fifty to sixty hours a week, for a job that provides them no benefits and no safety net. "They're gig workers," she explained.[49]

The creation of these kinds of sponsored posts is difficult, time-consuming work. Meg Conley, who has around 15,600 Instagram followers, describes a summer 2021 social media campaign she was asked to participate in. The ad would be for an ice cream company, as July 8 is apparently a made-up nonsense occasion called "National Freezer Pop Day." If you wanted to be included as an influencer in this campaign, "you had to complete its tasks," Conley explains:

> Promoting a coupon, creating an original Instagram story about the ice cream product, and an original Instagram post for the product. This content had to be sent to the campaign manager for approval before posting. This may not sound like a lot of work, but it is. Especially if you're a young mother with kids. It means staging an editorial photoshoot in your own home with an unruly crew.
>
> A shoot about ice cream pops will get more engagement if you do one of three things:
>
> 1. Your kids are in the IG post and story
> 2. You are in it, eating the pop, dressed well, with nails, hair and makeup done
> 3. You are sitting behind a pile of laundry, wryly eating the pop instead of doing your "actual" work.

Incredible bonus points of engagement are awarded to anyone who can figure out how to compose a photo including all three elements.[50]

As Conley points out, it is a delicious irony that in what she calls "the Exhibitor Economy," you can be compensated for the performance of care work, but not for the actual care work itself.

Jo Piazza estimates that she has talked to five hundred successful influencers for her podcast, and she said the vast majority of them find the performance really difficult. "There is a very small percentage who just love it, and it doesn't take anything from them. It's the same percentage that's stoked to be a celebrity—they love the performative nature of it," she said. For everyone else, "there's a part of it that crushes their soul every day to create the perfect image of motherhood that brands require in order to get paid."

Piazza said that it's an "open secret" in the influencer world that you need a perfect blowout and fake eyelashes in every picture, and "the perfect white kitchen and bedroom. You're not getting paid unless you're showing the aspirational view that brands have been peddling for fifty years."[51]

And the inequities in who is compensated for the performance are the same as everywhere else in motherhood. As Denene Millner put it to me, the people at the companies who decide how to spend their marketing budgets are still mostly white. "You go for what you know, and you go for what you think will sell to the widest audiences, and people think the widest audience is the white audience, but only because they're not catering to anything outside of what they already know. It's really fucking lazy and it's steeped in racism," she said.[52]

Millner agreed with Kathryn Jezer-Morton's assessment that the motherhood-influencer space is one of the least diverse on the internet. Marketers "look at Black mothers and see pathology and stereotype," she said, not an "aspirational" lifestyle.

And when moms of color are included, they may be compensated

at lower rates. While there isn't clear data about compensation—
we don't know what goes on behind the scenes unless the creators
themselves or the sponsoring companies tell us, and many sponsoring companies put nondisclosure agreements in their contracts—
Black TikTok creators have staged boycotts over the lack of credit
and compensation their work receives compared to their white counterparts.[53]

Emily Feret, twenty-nine, who goes by @emilyjeanne333 on
TikTok, has 867,500 followers and 18.3 million likes, as of January
2022. Even with this large following, and the fact that her more popular videos get over 100,000 views, she isn't making a ton of money.
"It's not enough to live off, it's some extra fun money," she said. She's
a stay-at-home mom of two, and she makes delightful and funny videos that send up the unattainable perfection that influencer moms
are selling.

In an effort to "normalize normalcy," Feret has done a series
of videos taking the viewer on a tour of her house. Narrating in a
slightly unhinged and extremely perky voice, she shows you "life
without the filter." Her two kids are always in the background, being
their normal tiny terrorist selves. "Levi, son, dear god, get out of the
trash can," she says with a smile. "Please stop going in there, you're
disgusting." Then she shows us her lamp, which is still in its original
plastic, and "There's dead bugs stuck in there!" she announces, before throwing her head back and laughing.[54]

"I'm a middle-class person. I don't have a nanny," Feret told me.
"If I'm making a video, it's shot in the natural light of my kitchen and
my kids are running around in it. Is that someone that a brand like
Nike or Target sees and says, 'I want to work with her'? Probably
not, because I don't fit that aesthetic that sells. It seems very filtered
and aesthetically pleasing and that's not what I'm representing."

She says her ultimate goal is to continue to reach more moms, to make them feel better about their lack of a perfect life. But to expand into YouTube, which is something she would like to do, she would need to make more money than just "fun money," because it would be a lot of work, and she's got her hands full with her two kids. There's a reason a lot of the most popular influencers are like Ree Drummond: they have enough money to have support while they work on building their empire.

Meg Conley obviously has no illusions about how the perfect influencer sausage is made. She has seen behind the curtain and knows how much work it takes, and that the image doesn't reflect reality. Her family moved to Oakland, California, after living in Utah, and it gave her some distance from the perfect influencer vision. Now she lives in Denver and tries to never engage with that kind of content. Most of the time, she's able to avoid it. But the Netflix show *Dream Home Makeover* was kicked up by the algorithm and she couldn't resist it.

Blond Brigham Young University graduate influencer and interior designer Shea McGee, who has three million followers on Instagram, hosts *Dream Home Makeover*. Echoing the language that many of the Mormon mom bloggers used about displaying the virtuous and lovely, McGee's website says, "In 2014, Shea and her husband Syd decided to launch their interior design firm with one directive in mind, 'Make Life Beautiful.'"[55] The McGees' Netflix series showcases their attractive family, and brings them into other families' homes to renovate. Their aesthetic is very white and very gold, and as Conley pointed out to me, the homes they renovate aren't "hovels." They are middle-class to upper-middle-class suburban abodes that the McGees turn into something "Instagram ready."

Watching the show made Conley panic so intensely she had to take an edible. "When I lived in Utah, that's how I felt. Because that coincided with Instagram starting to dominate. I was embarrassed of my life, and embarrassed of the spaces where I lived my life. I saw the way that women lived, because their lives were lived for presentation. I just hated myself," she said.[56]

Conley thought this way of living was losing relevance, so it bothers her that women like McGee are still considered so marketable that they are getting multimillion-dollar Netflix deals. She has three girls herself, and she wants them to see a vision of motherhood that is less confining than the one with which she was raised. When she sees McGee's perfect world elevated on one of the biggest streaming platforms in the world, she realizes: "This isn't just Provo priorities. That terrifies me."[57]

ANXIETY, JEALOUSY, SHAME, AND GUILT: THE FOUR HORSEMEN OF THE MOMPOCALYPSE

The impact of influencers on the psychological health of mothers also dismays Ilyse DiMarco, forty-three, a clinical psychologist and the author of *Mom Brain: Proven Strategies to Fight the Anxiety, Guilt, and Overwhelming Emotions of Motherhood—and Relax into Your New Self*. She treats lots of mothers who cite social media as one source of their anxiety, jealousy, shame, guilt, and mood issues, she said.

What strikes her in particular is that some of the moms who spiral from looking at the influencers on Instagram don't even *like* the influencers they are following or share their values, particularly. "My mom patients feel such shame and guilt and anxiety seeing what's going on with other people, even though they don't particularly respect them. It's such a driver of so many bad feelings."

Dr. DiMarco said that even as she helps mothers cope with the negative feelings they get from social media, she is not immune to those feelings herself. She has two boys, ten and seven, and even though she helps women build better social media habits, "it's still seductive."

Still, what she tries to impress upon her patients is "If you can find an influencer whose values you share and who provides you with helpful tips, great!" But if you are taking cues for living from influencers you don't respect, that's "like going to a doctor who you think is a quack, whose training you think is subpar, and then following their medical advice."[58]

And there is quite a lot of quackery out there. Brie M. Reid, who has a PhD in developmental psychology from the University of Minnesota's Institute of Child Development, calls the proliferation of bad advice the "weaponization" of research. Dr. Reid's research specializes in how toxic stress affects children across the life span, and so she knows firsthand that "there's such a wide range of parenting practices that result in a wide range of happy children, and most parents are doing the best they can in difficult circumstances."

Still, she sees a cohort of mothers online co-opting and misinterpreting research for their own ends. Specifically, some influencers cite studies about children who suffered from severe neglect in Romanian orphanages to suggest that parents shouldn't sleep train their kids.[59] If you aren't familiar with the Romanian orphanage story: A group of psychologists followed 136 Romanian babies for 14 years, starting in 2000. These orphans "laid in cribs all day, except when being fed, diapered or bathed on a set schedule. They weren't rocked or sung to. Many stared at their own hands, trying to derive whatever stimulation they could from the world around them."

Some—but crucially, not all—of these children would grow up to have "delays in cognitive function, motor development and language. They showed deficits in socio-emotional behaviors and experienced more psychiatric disorders." The children who were moved into loving foster families before the age of two showed almost no differences from the control group of children who had never been institutionalized.

It should go without saying that sleep training your children today has absolutely nothing to do with the issues of severely neglected Romanian orphans decades ago, Dr. Reid said.

Still, there are some moms like Sarah Ockwell-Smith, who calls herself a "gentle sleep training" expert, arguing that babies are incapable of self-soothing. She cites the Romanian sleep studies, and though she admits that it's an extreme example, Ockwell-Smith claims that sleep training will similarly thwart your baby's emotional development. Even though Ockwell-Smith admits there's no proof of this, she writes that "there is a potential correlation with sleep training" and sudden infant death syndrome.[60]

Dr. Reid is especially appalled, as a developmental child psychologist, to see the research around sleep used as a cudgel this way, "because sleep is so important developmentally for children and emotionally and physically for parents, especially for moms,"[61] and there is good evidence that poor sleep quality in new mothers is linked to greater incidence of postpartum depression.[62]

Despite these negative examples, I'm not trying to argue that the internet is wrong and bad—I love the internet! As previously stated, I wouldn't have a career without the internet. I have spent, conservatively, ten thousand hours watching TikTok videos. And yet I'm a trash monster by nature and probably need better boundaries when it comes to my social media consumption.

In her practice, Dr. DiMarco gives her clients the same basic advice that we can all use to forge healthy relationships with our social media use. First, if someone's content is making you feel bad, make a pros and cons list about following them. If following them generates more negativity than positivity, just unfollow or mute them.

Second, "Please actively pick a mom, or two or three," she said—

even better if it's in real life, but online is okay, too—whose opinions you truly value, and trust, and who don't make you feel like a dumpster fire. "Maybe they have slightly older kids, and they've been through it before. Consciously use those moms, ask them for advice," Dr. DiMarco said.

That said, the social media comparison got really out of control for a lot of people during the pandemic. "We all turned to social media for our socializing," said Dr. DiMarco, it was our only way to connect. All our old coping mechanisms online—and the entire scaffolding of our lives—were totally ripped to shreds in the course of a week. And we're still trying to figure out how to move forward.

SIX

Everything Falls Apart

CELEBRATING MY BIRTHDAY WITH
A KLONOPIN PRESCRIPTION

Everyone in the world probably has a series of moments when they realized the pandemic was going to dramatically alter their lives. I was still in denial at the beginning of March, when schools began to close in Washington State, where the first US COVID-19 cases were discovered.[1] Washington is three thousand miles away, I thought. At that point, all the extant cases in the United States were linked to international travelers, or were from American citizens on that cursed cruise ship.[2] I hadn't been abroad for years. It would be contained, I thought, like that case of Ebola in 2014.[3]

It became more real with each passing day. I remember the first time I called Sean O'Leary, a Colorado pediatrician who is on the American Academy of Pediatrics' Committee on Infectious Diseases, for an interview. It was Monday, March 9. I was sitting in a windowless conference room in my office, a small enclosed box a colleague once described as "breathy" because it would get hot with stale air during any meeting longer than fifteen minutes.

I can't remember the specific details of my conversation with Dr. O'Leary, but I'm sure none of the news was good. Shortly afterward, my boss sent an email to all her direct reports telling us that for the near term, we did not have to come into the office.

I was still nominally keeping it together as that week went on, but with each passing day my panic increased. School was still open for my kids, but people I knew were starting to pull their children out. On Tuesday, I thought they were nuts. By Friday morning, I wondered if I was making a huge mistake by sending my children in. My older daughter went to public school in a hundred-year-old building that showed its historic character and its grime. My younger daughter went to a three-room preschool that was in a newer building, but the kids were crawling all over each other, and one of the rooms had no windows.

I was a block away from my younger daughter's preschool that Friday morning when I looked down at my phone and realized they had sent a note asking anyone who *could* keep their children home, to please do so. I dropped her off, feeling horrible. But our older daughter was already at school and I felt paralyzed; I still had deadlines to meet, and I couldn't upend my carefully constructed care system before I absolutely had to.

I felt totally ill-equipped to be making any of these decisions, and I was despairing that they were left up to me as an individual parent. I had started calling Dr. O'Leary every single day for my reporting, so in some ways I was better armed to make choices for my family than almost anyone, and *still* I didn't know the right thing to do. The shaming and counter-shaming on the local mom Facebook groups just made it worse; you were either a monster for sending your kids to school, or a paranoid hypochondriac for pulling them out and depriving them of their education.

Just two days later, schools were shuttered; at the time, they said they'd be closed through April 20, but a wise colleague who had previously reported from war zones told me that if schools closed, they'd be shut for the rest of the school year. She knew from experience what it felt like when things were about to fall apart. That schools would be closed for months was a possibility I had never entertained, and one I still did not want to believe. It was my thirty-eighth birthday, and I celebrated by asking my psychiatrist for a Klonopin prescription.

I also remember posting happy photos of my family outside in our building's courtyard on that day because I am a hypocrite. I was supposed to be going on a sorely needed girls' trip with my best friend. Instead, I played hopscotch with my daughters in 30-degree weather, drawing the squares with sidewalk chalk. We are all smiling in the photo, and I wrote some faux cheerful caption about how the girls were social distancing like champs. I wonder if I was just trying to convince myself that everything was okay by projecting this snapshot, even though inside I was dying. Lots of other parents in my circle were doing the same thing: posting little snapshots of isolated hikes and midday baking experiments to find tiny moments of connection and positivity when it felt like everything around us was dissolving.

We muddled through that first week of remote learning. Because I am a type-A nutjob, I tried to make a strict schedule of activities, and my husband and I negotiated a fair trade-off of childcare. I can't recall how closely my kids adhered to that schedule, but I do remember doing cosmic yoga with them in our living room.

COVID-19 was spreading aggressively in New York by then. I broke the news that the New York City Parks Department does not clean or disinfect playground equipment, right before they closed the playgrounds. Our nanny and her daughter stopped coming—we were all too scared of infecting each other. The building I live in is next door to a nursing home, where fifty-five seniors would be dead by mid-April.[4]

We were afraid to go outside; the weather remained cold and unforgiving. Nothing felt sturdy under my feet, and I was only sleeping because I took half a Klonopin every night, the minute my children were in bed. Each morning I would wake up groggy and, for a minute, forget why my heart was beating rapidly; my body remembered to be afraid before my mind did.

The first thing I did after I opened my eyes on Monday, March 23, was to reach for the phone at my bedside. I wanted to see if any of my infectious disease sources had been in touch. Instead, there was an email from my father to say that my mother had a fever, cough, and shaking chills, and that she likely had the virus. Since both my parents are retired physicians, the news was imparted in a rather bloodless, clinical way.

Because I was reporting on the virus, I was following all the news closely. I knew that the fatality rate for people over seventy with COVID-19 was almost 9 percent, and despite my dad's calm delivery, I wanted to vomit.[5] I had several colleagues who had the virus by then; they had gotten it when there was massive community transfer in New York before quarantine. The boyfriend of one of them was in the hospital with it, and he was an otherwise healthy thirtysomething.

Two days later, my dad started getting sick. My mother's case of coronavirus was confirmed by a blood test that week, but she was already on the mend. Her fever was gone, she said—though she couldn't know for sure because somehow my doctor parents hadn't owned a thermometer for thirty years, and they were sold out everywhere. She had a lingering cough and remained exhausted, but she seemed destined to ride the illness out at home.

My dad was another story. His aches were so painful that he couldn't sleep. His chills were so bad that he shook the bed. He'd be okay for twelve or eighteen hours, and Tylenol helped, but whenever it wore off his symptoms would come rushing back. He would have a good day, able to stand upright long enough to take the dog out to do her business, but then the next day he'd be back in bed.

When I expressed alarm that his symptoms kept resurging, my parents brushed it off. I tried to offer them help—food, a thermometer, anything—but they refused it.

"We really don't need anything," my mother insisted. I stared at them through the screen. They were sitting upright next to each other at the kitchen table, but my dad looked as if he had been plucked out of a drain.

We hid their illness from our children because we didn't want to scare them. Even our then three-year-old knew about "the germ"— her preschool had written little books for the kids, trying to explain coronavirus to them. "Every day is a home day" is the line from it that my husband and I would repeat to each other, like a mantra, a joke that wasn't really funny.

Meanwhile, our older daughter started having daily meltdowns. The apps she needed to use for her schoolwork didn't work very well, and she would become panicked at the thought that she could not file her work on time or in the correct way. She is tightly wound like me, and my heart broke for her.

Our little one was glued to our sides. I remember doing a video interview of a potential hire, and though I was trying to project professionalism, my daughter wouldn't stop coming into my bedroom, the only place with a closed door where I could reliably work. Finally, I told her she could stay in the room with me as long as she was quiet, and my call was so boring for her she quickly fell asleep next to me. It would be one of the few times she napped during quarantine.

My husband and I were both trying to do our full-time jobs and manage our children's various Zooms and navigate the janky learning apps and support them emotionally. My meticulous schedule from the first week was in shambles, except for waking up, breakfast, lunch, and dinner. We still ate our meals together and tried to wake up and go to sleep at roughly the usual times, though sleep never came easily for me.

My husband and I decided that I would be the one to get groceries when we needed them. This was both selfish and practical; the death rates were much higher for men, I reasoned, so if one of us was going to get infected, it should be me. But I also needed that time out of the house so that I could cry. It was the only time I could be completely alone.

Despite how difficult our lives felt in March and April 2020, we knew even at the time that we had it comparatively easy. I was reporting from the comfort of my home; I could keep my job without leaving the house and risking exposure, and my husband could keep his job, too. We had enough money to support ourselves. I had a true partner in my husband, who did more than his fair share of kid wrangling.

I was interviewing mothers who couldn't afford diapers, formula, and wipes for their kids, and talking to diaper bank administrators about the massive uptick in need because of pandemic-related job loss as entire public-facing industries abruptly shuttered. When I hustled through the supermarket aisles on my single weekly journey to the grocery store, I saw all the baby supplies had been cleaned out, so even parents who could afford those supplies might be left hanging because of panic buying. I was grateful to not have a newborn.

I was also talking to mothers every single day—both professionally and personally—who were not getting any help at all, domestically. Some of them were single parents, left without their villages. Others were married or partnered, and their spouses were either essential workers who were out of the house, or just couldn't be bothered to sacrifice the sanctity of their jobs for their families in crisis. The data showed how truly unusual my husband was in terms of his partnership; I will never forget the headline from my colleague Claire Cain Miller's piece in May 2020: "Nearly Half of Men Say They Do Most of the Home Schooling. 3 Percent of Women Agree."[6]

The numbers from the American Time Use Survey (ATUS), which tracks the number of minutes the average American spends doing particular tasks, showed that for the year 2020, "parents with school-aged children spent an average of 1.6 hours more a day providing 'secondary childcare'—time spent taking care of children while also doing other things, such as working," than they did in 2019. And mothers of school-age children spent significantly more time doing childcare than fathers did: moms spent over seven hours a day caring for children, compared to less than five for dads, according to analysis of the ATUS numbers by journalists Ben Casselman and Ella Koeze.[7]

Everything ground to a halt when the quarantines began, in a way most Americans had never experienced. This could have been a moment where families and communities reassessed and supported mothers; our intimate relationships could have been restructured to suit everyone's needs better. But instead, much of the additional domestic work required when schools, day care, and family caretaking systems fell apart was left to mothers. And despite the fact that things have improved somewhat for mothers up and down the economic spectrum since the nadir of the pandemic in 2020, the economic and emotional fallout is still disproportionately affecting them. Many mothers continue to feel as if they are being forced to make a choice between their family's health and well-being and their ability to afford basic needs.

DISASTER DOMESTICITY

Initially, it may have seemed like the economic fallout of the pandemic was felt equally by those in the industries decimated by quarantine, mostly in the service sectors. Restaurants, salons, and hotels were required to shutter for weeks if not months, depending on local laws, and millions of people were laid off. In April 2020 alone, over twenty million people lost their jobs, and the jump in unemployment was the highest in the recorded history of the US Bureau of Labor Statistics.[8] The labor force participation levels were at their lowest rates in almost fifty years.

While these job losses were (and in some cases, continue to be) devastating for many people regardless of parental status, if you dig into the numbers, you find that layoffs affected fathers less than everyone else during the early part of the pandemic, something sociologists call "the fatherhood premium." After controlling for race, education, and age, for mothers and the child-free of any gender, the layoff rate between March and May 2020 was roughly equal, between 10 and 11 percent. For fathers, the layoff rate was only 6.8 percentage points. "Cultural beliefs of mothers as expressive caretakers and fathers as active breadwinners and deserving of career advancement may shape employers' decisions," according to researchers who studied the layoff gap.[9]

This initial ripple of the enforcement of traditional gender roles would become a whirlpool, sucking mothers down as the pandemic wore on. While some mothers were laid off, others made the "choice" to leave paid work, a choice made under duress when there were no other options for childcare or education. In March and April 2020, 45 percent of mothers of school-age children were not working. That percentage had declined by January 2021, but there were still 1.4 million more mothers out of paid work than there had been before the pandemic, in January 2020. Non-white single mothers were hit the hardest, according to analysis of Census Bureau data.[10]

At the beginning of the pandemic, I remember one of my mom friends joking that COVID-19 was just a plot by traditionalists to get women back into the kitchen, and she turned out to be a little psychic. Not only was an enforced disaster domesticity the outcome for many mothers, but some attitudes toward gender roles actually went back in time.

Why did we revert to these stereotypes, so quickly and so automatically? "One simple answer is, we had these gender roles that were already there," said Leah Ruppanner, a professor of sociology and a director at the Future of Work Lab at the University of Melbourne in Australia. Which is to say, mothers were already doing more of the childcare and homemaking, and the perfect domestic ideals we've internalized were already inside us, so why not just double down on the path of least resistance?

Even before the pandemic, every year labor force participation went down for mothers in the summer: moms of young children were more likely to be out of work when school was out because childcare is expensive and hard to come by. When schools shuttered in the spring, "People went into crisis mode and went back to those default gender roles," Ruppanner said.[11]

One study collected data from over fifteen hundred people on attitudes toward mothers' and fathers' roles in August 2019 and then again in August 2020. In August 2020, the majority of opinions about how parents should behave became much more retro:

> Several traditional gender role attitudes gained support. The largest shifts show increased support of fathers as disciplinarians and mothers as schedulers for their children. There were also significant decreases in agreement that it is essential for fathers to play with their children and that they should spend less time working. Furthermore, there were significant increases in agreement that mothers are happier at home, should not work when they have young children, and should usually stay home.[12]

The only nontraditional attitude in August 2020 was that there was more support for both mothers and fathers earning money. This combination of expectations—mothers should earn money but also stay home with young children—is actually the worst of all possible worlds. Patrice Gamble, who is the twenty-seven-year-old mom of a two-year-old, has been working from home the whole time, with little help, as her partner is a tow truck driver and had to be at work in person. Her working hours are unsustainable because she is also trying to care for her son without much support.

"I may be leading a call but my son is having a fit. Then I get comments like, 'You're doing great, but you seem to be distracted on calls.' Of course I am distracted, I'm working from home with a kid," she said when I spoke to her in June 2021. Patrice is not a fan of the work-from-home environment—she gets all her work done, but she's under constant stress about her child's needs and is getting very little sleep.[13] Her coworkers try to be empathetic, but they don't have children, so they don't really understand the pressure she's under.

Misty Heggeness, the principal economist and senior adviser at the US Census Bureau, said that at this point in the pandemic—the summer of 2021—moms like Patrice, who are in dual-income households and can telework, were more likely to have dropped out of the workforce because of COVID-19 than fathers or child-free people who were able to telework. "If you were in a teleworkable job, our a priori thinking is telework is so great for mothers because it allows for more flexibility, and more of them will be able to keep their jobs because of that flexibility," but what the data show is that when compared to women without children who could telework, more moms who *could* work from home quit.

Heggeness, who was a teleworking mom herself, said, "Every virtual school break, my children were in my office, sitting on the floor. They're bored, they're hungry, they want a snack. All their emotional needs are very distracting . . . I think I burnt out two dozen times throughout this whole experience, it's too much."[14]

Still, it's not like the picture is much rosier for essential worker moms who have had to go back into a physical workplace. For one, many of them are still in debt from the loss of income during the darkest days of quarantine, like Dreama James, the fast-food worker in Georgia who is still reeling from the credit card debt she accrued in 2020.[15]

Though there has been some federal support from disaster relief programs from both the Trump and Biden administrations, most families find that it's not enough to really move the needle. Michael Madowitz, a senior economist for the Joint Economic Committee Democrats, said, "The idea that a few hundred dollars a month will bring parents from not affording childcare to affording childcare strikes me as a reach."[16] The $300 a month, which is the maximum that parents get for children under six through the American Rescue Plan,[17] would pay for about a week of childcare in a high-quality center,[18] or a few months' supply of diapers and wipes.

An ongoing study out of the University of Oregon of parents of young children, called the Rapid-EC Study, found that one in four families has overdue debt or unpaid bills—and more than half of these parents reported increased debt compared to before the pandemic.[19] "I am working full-time and we are trying. I have debts that cause me so much anxiety sometimes I just cry alone in the car or shower," one New Jersey respondent told researchers.

Economic stressors have a direct impact on the mental health of both parents and children. When parents are financially strapped and unable to meet their children's basic needs, they become more stressed and anxious, and that anxiety affects their kids, too. The authors of the Rapid-EC Study called it a "Hardship Chain Reaction." Roughly 20 percent of parents of young children surveyed early on in the pandemic had trouble paying for their kids' food and shelter, and that 20 percent was disproportionately Black and Latino.[20]

Beyond financial stresses, moms were torn apart emotionally by the increase in their "second shift" work; in addition to the second shift of domestic responsibilities, distance learning became a third shift, and working, parenting, and education became an unsustainable twenty-four-hour-a-day job. Countless women told me stories of sleeping only four to five hours a night in order to get done everything that was asked of them.

AMERICAN MOMS ARE
STILL STRESSED

Since the beginning of the pandemic, research has shown that parents of children under eighteen have been more stressed and anxious than the child-free. According to a survey done by the American Psychological Association in April and May 2020, the average reported stress level for parents was a 6.7 on a 10-point scale, where 1 means "little or no stress" and 10 means "a great deal of stress." For everyone else, stress levels were at a 5.5. Almost half of parents said their stress level was high, compared with just 28 percent of adults without children.[21]

The levels of stress may also be worse for American mothers than for mothers of peer nations. Leah Ruppanner and her colleagues compared stress levels of American parents during the pandemic with stress levels of Australian parents, and found that American mothers were the most emotionally impacted. As that study concluded: "U.S. mothers, in particular, experienced distinct cross-cutting disadvantage from job loss and increases in housework on financial worry and emotional strain that were distinct to other groups."[22]

Philip Fisher, a professor of psychology at the University of Oregon who runs the Rapid-EC project, told me that in addition to economic distress, the study showed that two other factors really increased mental health issues for moms. One was that when the new school year rolled around in the late summer and early fall of 2020, the vast majority of parents were doing remote learning all on their own without any help.[23]

The other was that the women who were forced to leave their jobs or cut back on hours to help with remote learning were really unhappy about it. "Being forced to stop or reduce working took an emotional toll on moms," Fisher told me, and these moms were cutting back on work whether they could afford to do it or not (82 percent of them could not).[24] As Leah Ruppanner's research has shown, unsurprisingly, there's a direct relationship between school closures and mothers leaving or cutting back on work.[25]

The forces pushing mothers out of paid work were both external—coming from gendered wage gaps and cultural ideals about male breadwinners—and internal. In a qualitative study of heterosexual married parents in Indiana, the sociologist Jessica Calarco and her coauthors found that:

> Mothers (and fathers) justified unequal parenting arrangements by pointing to gendered structural and cultural conditions that made mothers' disproportionate labor seem "practical" and "natural." These justifications allowed couples to rely on mothers by default rather than through active negotiation. As a result, many mothers did not feel entitled to seek support with childcare from fathers or non-parental caregivers and experienced guilt if they did so.[26]

A California mom I will call Amelia is representative of everything described above. She is a forty-seven-year-old mom of two kids who are eight and six; her older child has an individualized education plan and his educational needs are big enough that before the pandemic, his public school had assigned him paraprofessional aid to give him one-on-one attention. He was also receiving occupational therapy.

Amelia is an appellate public defender who defends parents whose kids were removed from their homes and placed in foster care. She also works on some juvenile criminal public defense cases. In California, this is a contract role with the state, so she does not have benefits, and if she doesn't work, she does not get paid.

When schools closed in March 2020, her career was "totally put on hold." Her husband's job provides the family benefits and is less flexible than hers, so her job took the hit. Her son was in first grade then, and she had to sit with him for every single Zoom. In the summer, her kids went to camp, and that was "amazing," she said.

Amelia used the time to figure out whether it would be financially better for the family if she went on unemployment or if she got a Paycheck Protection Program loan—a type of COVID-19 relief payment offered by the Small Business Administration that ended on May 31, 2021.[27] She said navigating those public systems took an "unbelievable" amount of time, and although she did get a PPP loan, she ultimately had to go on unemployment for part of the pandemic.

She assumed her kids would return to in-person school in August 2020 and was shocked when her district announced they would be fully remote indefinitely. She and her husband got their kids into a YMCA learning camp that would support both their kids, which they felt lucky to get into; but the cost of the program was a deep strain on them financially. Amelia still had to be much more involved with her kids' learning than she was before the pandemic, so she couldn't take on extra work to make ends meet.

"They threw special ed kids under the bus," she said. "It felt like my other part-time job was just trying to stay on top of his services, fighting with the school district, trying to get legal help from whoever I could. It was awful."

Amelia was also devastated to have to cut back on work during the pandemic. "I have been working part time, and on and off unemployment. I don't want to be on unemployment, I want to be working. I have been doing this job for a long time and I love it. I'm not a paraprofessional or a teacher, and I was left flailing and not able to do the job that I love and am qualified for, and unable to help the parents and families that need me as a public defender. I'm really angry about it." During the periods she was taking on some work, she was waking up at 4:00 or 5:00 a.m. every day to get it done while still supporting her kids, who did not return to in-person school until April 2021. "Emotionally, it's been pretty stressful and bad. I have had very little personal time," she said.[28]

A lot of moms I have interviewed have found that this lack of personal time means that their pre-pandemic coping mechanisms are not available to them, which makes them feel more stressed and less able to deal with the pressures of work and care stacked on top of each other.

Malinda Ann Hill, fifty, who is a single mom to an eighteen-year-old daughter, was already contemplating going into serious therapy for an eating disorder when the pandemic hit. She is the bereavement coordinator at Children's Hospital of Philadelphia, and "the emotional toll of the pandemic on our families pushed me over the edge," she told me. She ended up having to take a leave from her job to do an immersive online therapy program, and disability did not pay her full salary. She returned to her job in July 2020, but did not feel ready—it was just financially imperative.

The stress and sadness were overwhelming. "I worked myself into another relapse," she said. She started having panic attacks whenever she had to go outside; the symptoms of her eating disorder ramped up; and she had to return to another virtual therapy program in March 2021. Her daughter, who was at that point a senior in high school, was also experiencing anxiety and depression as a result of the pandemic and started seeing her own therapist. "I'm grateful she reached out to me about that," Malinda said.

"I have been able to hold it together for eighteen years as a single mom," she said, but having to deal with death all the time as part of her job, and then to watch it happen on a global scale, was too much to bear. "I was already on the verge of burning out, and you couldn't escape death, it was everywhere." Because of the amount of disability she has taken over the past two years, Malinda is moving out of her current apartment into something cheaper. "My savings has dwindled significantly. I have no other choice," she said. "I have to take care of myself and it is one day at a time."[29]

Stay-at-home moms are also dealing with extreme levels of over-whelm. For some, their domestic load doubled with their kids never leaving the house. And as their spouses had to keep working to support their families outside the home during the day, their breaks were few.

Theresa Peters, forty-one, who lives in Anchorage, Alaska, had three kids under twelve when the pandemic started. Because Alaska is so isolated, and the weather is often so cold, "My coping mechanisms for parenting often involved getting away from the home or my children at intervals of the year for a short break by traveling to see friends. I have not been able to travel safely for the last two years," she said. Her husband works full time in construction as an essential worker, and he is out of the house for long hours, leaving her alone with the kids.

Theresa feels that many people in her community still do not take the virus seriously, and she worries about her children's health, and despairs that the sacrifices she has made will be for naught. "I am living on a thread of sanity and the result of my stress and absolute disgust with the world right now have done nothing to calm me or assure me that things will get better," she said.

Theresa has a son with autism, and as with Amelia's son with special needs, distance learning was extremely hard on him. Theresa had to monitor his classes, while also trying to help her kindergartner with distance learning because she was too little to do it on her own. Her middle child was the only one who could manage school all by himself. She also had to keep the house in order and cook the meals, and she was trying to take in some writing and illustrating work to generate extra income for her family.

Though her children returned to at least some in-person school in January 2021, the cumulative effect of the pandemic and its uncertainties has taken a long-term toll on Theresa's mental health. Before COVID-19 she had suffered bouts of depression, but "I was never this anxious before. The last couple of years have made me more afraid of the public, more afraid of going places, more afraid of everything. I freak out with every little thing. I was never this way before . . . I love my children, but in retrospect, I always feel like I'm not doing it right."[30]

Amelia and Theresa are not alone in their struggles. Parents of special needs children have reported lower levels of emotional well-being than parents whose children do not have special needs, according to the Rapid-EC project. These elevated levels of distress have been significant and unchanged since the beginning of the pandemic.[31] Children with special needs were not well served by distance learning, leading to parents across the country suing their state's department of education, arguing that the individualized education plan their child is entitled to was not followed.[32]

Although K through 12 public schools are required to educate all children, it is much harder to find care for young children with special needs. Even before the pandemic, it was a struggle for parents to find high-quality, affordable childcare for children with autism and other disabilities.[33] Children with behavioral challenges would often get kicked out of care situations that were not equipped to deal with their issues.

During the pandemic, the availability of care for children with disabilities was even harder to come by for the 5.7 million children under six with at least one functional difficulty.[34] As a parent in Georgia told the Rapid-EC survey, "They need to send out more money. They don't realize the impact this has on families with special needs children. When day care programs are closed and the special needs school program is only open two days a week, and you can't find someone to watch your child while you work, you can't earn the money to pay the bills. We need more support with housing. It's impossible sometimes."[35]

For all families of young children, the fact that childcare is not back to where it was before the pandemic is a major problem. Amelia is despairing that even though her children are supposed to be going back to in-person school this fall, they cannot find aftercare. She said, before the pandemic, "at our school we had about two hundred kids in aftercare. The latest I heard there were twenty-eight spots" for fall 2021. School gets out at two. Amelia can't afford to stop working indefinitely—her family needs the income. But she also can't get care—she could barely afford the care available during the 2020–21 school year. Like so many other American mothers, she is trapped.

CHILDCARE BREAKDOWN

The American childcare system was already in such bad shape before the pandemic that some experts I spoke to wouldn't even call it a "system." It's a patchwork of individual and local solutions that are either egregiously expensive or low quality. According to the

2019 annual report from the organization Child Care Aware, the US Department of Health and Human Services recommends that low-income people pay no more than 7 percent of their earnings in childcare; and yet "in eight states plus the District of Columbia, childcare prices for center-based infant care cost millennial parents over 35 percent of average income."[36]

Children from the poorest families receive some childcare support funding from the federal government. The funding from the federal government is distributed to parents through block grants given to individual states. According to a Child Care Aware report, before the pandemic "only two million of the 13.6 million children who met federal eligibility requirements for childcare subsidies actually received those subsidies." That's one in seven.[37]

Even for families who can afford the exceedingly high cost of care, it is often hard to come by. I have heard about parents putting their children on day-care waitlists as soon as the pee stick was positive, and not receiving spots until their child was over one. Poor families have a different problem; often in low-income areas, residents cannot afford the cost of high-quality care, and so reputable centers can't stay open because they can't get the funding.

Experts coined the term "childcare deserts" to describe areas of the country where the number of children who need care is much higher than the available spots. According to a report from the Center for American Progress from 2018, "among parents with a child under age five, 83 percent reported that finding quality, affordable childcare was a serious problem in their area."[38]

The same report found that nearly half the neighborhoods in the United States do not have an adequate supply of licensed childcare options. For example, the North Country—a rural area of northern New York State—had an estimated 60,000 children from 0 to 11 years old, and only 10,058 regulated childcare spots in 2019. A whopping 78 percent of households said they had work issues, including missing shifts, late arrivals or early departures, lost pay, or even quitting jobs because of childcare needs.[39]

The pandemic destabilized our already ramshackle structures of childcare. Although relief funding from the Paycheck Protection Program was able to keep a good chunk of centers from closing during the early days of the COVID-19 crisis, 80 percent of childcare centers are experiencing staffing shortages, a third have longer wait lists than pre-pandemic, and about a quarter have reduced their operating hours.[40]

Audrey, a single mom who was living in Los Angeles at the beginning of COVID-19, saw her day care—which she waited a year to get her toddler son into—permanently close during the pandemic. She was ultimately forced to move in with her parents in the suburbs because when quarantine began, she was four weeks into a new job she could not afford to lose, and she needed at least some childcare help.

Although she was able to find a new day care in the suburbs in the summer of 2020, Audrey is still working around the clock to support her family; most weekdays, she wakes up at 4:00 a.m. to start work, and isn't asleep until midnight. "I have lost twenty pounds from stress," she said.

Her son's father has repeatedly harassed her during the pandemic, and she has had to get a restraining order against him. Her ex is also anti-vaccine, and she had to go to court to be able to get their child a flu shot. Her childcare support hearing was delayed more than a year because of the pandemic, and it was just beginning to get sorted when I spoke to her for the second time in early 2022. Even though Audrey has been promoted at work, she wonders at what cost. "The toll and stress has been unbearable," she said. "I feel robbed of what motherhood was supposed to be like."[41]

For parents who have childcare, the risk of COVID-19 closures going forward creates a great deal of stress. "Day care is shutting down when there is any concern of exposure, and I don't have the ability to take that much time off work," one Pennsylvania mom told the Rapid-EC project when asked to describe her biggest current challenges. "Also contributing to stress are the MANY hospital bills from when I got Covid that have been sent to collections and now I'm being harassed via phone and mail by collection agencies," she added.[42]

Many, many studies across different fields have shown that inadequate childcare is not just a problem for individual mothers and families; it is also a problem for society. Because parents cannot remain in steady work without childcare, economically, the country is losing out on billions of dollars, according to research from the US Chamber of Commerce Foundation. For example, before the pandemic, Pennsylvania alone was losing $3.47 billion annually in tax revenue and employee absences and turnover because of childcare breakdowns.[43]

But even more destructive to the fabric of society is the effect of inadequate systems of care and education for our children. The greatest amount of brain development happens in the first years of a child's life. For the under-three set, a lack of responsive, nurturing, high-quality care can have lifelong ramifications. According to a 2021 report from the nonprofit organization Zero to Three, which focuses on the health of infants and toddlers, "Babies who experience fewer nurturing and high-quality interactions are at risk of having their brain development damaged or delayed, with severe consequences for the rest of their lives."[44]

Forty-nine out of fifty states do not meet the ideal caregiver-to-child ratio established by the federal Head Start program for all children under three. Using Texas as an example: "At eleven months, a child in Texas shares their caregiver with, at most, three other infants. However, at nineteen months, the same Texan child might suddenly share their caregiver with a group of eight other toddlers, more than twice the Early Head Start ratio. At thirty months, this Texan child could share their caregiver with ten other babies, nearly three times higher than the Early Head Start ratio of 1:4," according to Zero to Three.[45]

Patricia Cole, the senior director of federal policy at Zero to Three, said the worst part of the unending nature of the pandemic for mothers and their babies is the precariousness of their circumstances. "Stimulus payments came and went, unemployment insurance rose and fell, and finally the enhanced Child Tax Credit came and went," Cole said. "That unpredictability increases the stress above and beyond what you would have from material hardship and overall stress from the pandemic."

Cole said that another problem is when care does not match up with job gain and loss for primary caretakers. Let's say a mom worked in retail, and she lost her job during that first COVID-19 shutdown. She might have had her job return, but her day care never reopened; or, she got a new job, got the day care, and then got laid off. She can't afford that childcare she lined up, and she can't look for a new job without childcare.[46] According to research from Zero to Three, "The constant juggling of work schedules and family needs can lead to depression and stress in parents and caregivers and a home environment of increased instability and chaos."[47]

While the costs of childcare decrease for most families as their children get older, and eventually most kids can be left at home without supervision, the pandemic has also affected the mental and physical health of older children, and the stress of overseeing remote school has taken its toll on many families. There's a cliché that mothers are only as happy as their least happy child, and the mothers of many teenagers going through painful pandemics are very unhappy indeed.

"FOR MY SON, THERE WAS NO NORMAL"

Tanya Ilela, fifty-one, who is from the Denver area, saw how difficult the pandemic has been for teenagers from both a personal and a professional perspective. She's a single mom of three kids, a fourteen-year-old boy, an eighteen-year-old boy, and a twenty-two-year-old-girl, and she's also a high school counselor. "I work in a school where there's a lot of low-income students. Those kids were trying to navigate an eight-hour day, and oftentimes an eight-hour job, and then having to be responsible for their parents or dealing with sickness, and they were in that weird space of shouldering the adult responsibilities," she said.

Looking at the numbers on learning loss, it's hard to say that the pandemic school year was anything but a disaster for many American families. Some students were kept out of school entirely, and they tended to be younger children from the most vulnerable populations. "More than one million children who had been expected to enroll in these schools did not show up, either in person or online. The missing students were concentrated in the younger grades, with the steepest drop in kindergarten—more than 340,000 students, according to government data," per analysis in the *New York Times* by Dana Goldstein and Alicia Parlapiano.[48]

For the children who did show up, students in grades 3 through 8 were 8 to 12 percentile points behind in math and 3 to 6 percentile points behind in reading than in a typical year, according to a July 2021 report from the NWEA, an educational research nonprofit. While learning levels were down among all groups, Black, Latino/ Hispanic, Native American, and impoverished students were disproportionately affected.[49]

In 2020, researchers at McKinsey estimated "that an additional 2 to 9 percent of high-school students could drop out as a result of the coronavirus and associated school closures—232,000 ninth-to-eleventh graders (in the mildest scenario) to 1.1 million (in the worst)."[50] Many students were also dealing with grief while trying to learn in difficult circumstances. Particularly in Black and Brown communities where there was a disproportionate amount of death from COVID-19,[51] children may have had to struggle through school after having lost parents or grandparents.

The mental health impact on children has been devastating for many. "My nine-year-old has been remote schooling for over a year and her school won't return this year," a North Carolina mother told the Rapid-EC project in May 2021. "This has caused her increasing anxiety to the point she is undergoing therapy and taking special medication. She has even had panic attacks. She misses normalcy and being around kids her age so much. I have done everything I could to help her, but I largely feel helpless. I can't wait until August when she will go back to school."[52]

It was very difficult for Tanya to parent under pandemic circumstances, and under the weight of the pain of the students she counsels. "For my son, there was no normal. I didn't even know how to relate or navigate it for him," she said of her eighteen-year-old. "I don't even know what to say. 'I'm sorry you don't have a prom, I'm sorry you don't have a graduation.' What do you say? Other than we're all in this together. And how do you give them hope? Because it didn't seem very hopeful, and I'm not sure it still even does."

Though Tanya is white, her children are biracial—their father is Black—and the death of George Floyd and its aftermath were also hard for them. They particularly identified with the local case of Elijah McClain, a Black twenty-three-year-old who died in 2019 "after the police in Aurora, Colo., restrained him with a chokehold that has since been banned," according to the *New York Times*.[53] McClain had simply been walking home from a convenience store when he was detained by police because someone had called 911 and said he "looked sketchy." Her sons especially felt "that could be me walking home."

Tanya attended protests with her children in the summer of 2020, but she knows that she does not have the same lived experiences as her kids. "My children have to live it as Black children in America, because they are darker skinned, and that's sometimes where I feel helpless," she said.[54]

Her children are far from alone; about half of Black Americans cite discrimination as a source of stress for them, more than any other racial group, according to the American Psychological Association. Furthermore, "the majority of adults (59 percent), regardless of race, report police violence toward minorities is a significant source of stress in their life. This is significantly higher than the 36 percent of adults who said the same in 2016 when this question was first asked," the APA reports.[55]

Teens have been particularly hard-hit by pandemic uncertainty; and Tanya is right that it is tough to encourage them to be hopeful. According to that same APA report, nearly 80 percent of young adults ages eighteen to twenty-three agreed with the statement: "The future of our nation is a significant source of stress in their life," and they reported being significantly more stressed than adults of any other age group.[56]

As the APA points out, youth do lack perspective, and so it may be easier for moms to have hope than it is for our teenagers. Tanya, for one, felt that there have been benefits for her during this pandemic—she's learned how to slow down in ways she never has before. "I had spent twenty-two years being a working mom, running my kids all over town for all the sports and activities and camps," she said. The pandemic made her tune into herself. She's been seeing a therapist, reconnecting with friends, and "taking time to intentionally feed myself," she said. She realized that her son might be playing a lot more video games than he did before the pandemic, but that doesn't mean he's not still an awesome kid who continues to do well in school under less than ideal circumstances.

Many moms I have spoken to since March 2020 echoed Tanya's sentiments, and they also relished the extra time they had with their children, even as they were often stressed. One respondent to the Rapid-EC study said, "While the fear and worry are awful, there have been bright spots. I've gotten to spend more time with my son during his first year than I thought I would. We have also spent more time with my parents and they've gotten to watch him grow every day."[57]

"IT WAS A MESS BEFORE YOU GOT HERE"

I have lost large chunks of spring 2020, but I remember a few things. I gave my whole family terrible haircuts. My daughters ate quesadillas for lunch every day for two weeks. We went to an area of rocks and a tiny beach overlooking the East River that I started calling "apocalypse playground."

The clearest snippet is the image of my dad, propped up by a pillow, playing chess with my older daughter over FaceTime. He still wasn't well—the bed-shaking chills and the fever persisted for three weeks when all was said and done. But on his better days he wanted to connect with his grandkids more than anything. And though he thinks his neurological symptoms and fatigue lasted for a few months after the acute illness, he survived.

Both my parents were tested a month after my dad's acute illness resolved, and they both had antibodies for COVID-19. In a messed-up way, this was a blessing; grandparents all over the country weren't allowed to see their grandkids for fear of getting sick, but my parents were immune and so could see our family without outsized worry.

Eventually we all moved in together so that we could have some childcare and support with distance learning. A few days into our multigenerational living arrangement, my mother asked my older daughter how remote school had been going. "It was a mess before you got here," my daughter told her.

I thought we would stay a few weeks—I didn't want to wear out our welcome, and the idea of living with my parents at thirty-eight did not thrill me. But it ended up suiting everyone so much that we stayed for months. My girls got help with remote school and true quality time with their grandparents. My husband and I got blocks of uninterrupted time to do our jobs; if we had not had this time, I think one of us would have had to take a leave from work. My parents got more company and more help with chores, and they cherished the additional closeness with my kids, who they got to know on a much more intimate level.

We were not only lucky that my parents survived the virus. We were doubly lucky that they were retired and otherwise healthy, and that they could shape their days around caretaking in a way we could not afford to. I also felt grateful that we had a good enough relationship that living together was a joy rather than a burden.

From a global perspective, the nuclear family living in an individual home is an anomaly, and even in the United States, the country has been moving away from that model for decades. At its nadir in 1970, twenty-six million people lived in multigenerational households. By 2008, that figure was at forty-nine million.[58] The pandemic accelerated this trend exponentially, and by September 2020, the majority of young adults were living with their parents for the first time since the Great Depression.[59] As a result, according to Brookings Institution analysis, "The so-called 'nuclear family' is no longer the dominant household structure."[60]

In a prescient *Atlantic* cover story published just as coronavirus was crashing over the United States, David Brooks boldly declared,

"The Nuclear Family Was a Mistake." Although I don't agree with all the analysis he offers in that piece, this part resonated:

> An extended family is one or more families in a supporting web. Your spouse and children come first, but there are also cousins, in-laws, grandparents—a complex web of relationships among, say, seven, ten, or twenty people. If a mother dies, siblings, uncles, aunts, and grandparents are there to step in. If a relationship between a father and a child ruptures, others can fill the breach. Extended families have more people to share the unexpected burdens—when a kid gets sick in the middle of the day or when an adult unexpectedly loses a job.
>
> A detached nuclear family, by contrast, is an intense set of relationships among, say, four people. If one relationship breaks, there are no shock absorbers.[61]

But there are shock absorbers—there have to be. The shock absorbers are the moms, and the stress they continue to experience as a result of the pandemic is untenable. Even before the pandemic, raising kids is too big and important a task to leave for just two parents without additional support. That's why we need to be offered help from our extended families, and we must ask for that help as well.

Extended family ties are essential to the well-being of mothers, but "family" doesn't necessarily have to be people you are related to by blood. The Rapid-EC project found that high levels of social support can be incredibly protective; even when families experienced economic hardship, if caregivers reported high levels of emotional support, they were much less likely to report stress. Up and down the socioeconomic ladder, "emotional supports interrupt the chain reaction from material hardship to child emotional distress."[62]

When she helps us out, my mother always says she's just doing what my oma and opa did for her; my grandparents lived thirty minutes away, and they saved my parents during many childcare fails. We decided to live with them again during the summer of 2021. Not out of panicked pandemic necessity, but because we missed each other. I don't want to go back to my siloed pre-pandemic life, and after watching my parents get COVID-19, I am excruciatingly aware that our time together will someday come to an end.

Though the pandemic has been very difficult, it has also inspired many of us. We have reassessed our lives and our closest ties, but we have also pushed out into the community and tried to make the world a better place for other families.

In the next chapter, we'll talk about the mothers fighting for changes big and small, and how, after decades of sluggish movement on social support that might help families, there is finally political energy behind real changes to the system. Though there is a long and dangerous road, filled with setbacks, to get to a more robust and permanent kind of support.

SEVEN

How Do We Make Meaningful Change?

A DOSE OF HOPE

I wrote the first draft of this chapter in early August 2021, as the more contagious Delta variant of the coronavirus enveloped the southern part of the United States and crept northward. My kids went to in-person day camp that summer, and dropping them off the first day in late June felt like taking a deep breath of ocean air after getting held under by a crashing wave. Their tantrums basically stopped and they slept like baby angels. All the adults in my family and close friends were vaccinated, all the counselors were vaccinated, and the local case rates remained low. I returned to the gym in person.

Six weeks later, the ecstasy of reprieve slipped away. There were two cases of COVID-19 at my children's camp. Luckily neither was in their groups, so we did not have to quarantine, but it was a reminder that the fall would bring continued interruptions to their education, despite our best efforts.

Indeed, now that I'm editing this chapter in December 2021, my kindergartner's class got shut down for a week in October because of a class outbreak—though thankfully she was spared. Both my children received their vaccinations in November, but as they reached peak immunity in early December, the Omicron variant came roaring into New York City, just in time to ruin the holidays.

I had tricked myself into thinking their remote year had been pretty decent because we are wealthy enough to pay for lots of extra support to help them navigate online public school, and they seemed to be doing okay emotionally. But seeing how blissfully happy my girls were at in-person camp, and how much happier they were to be back in person at school, just emphasized how much they had given up by missing normal school and life for fifteen months.

"Eradicating this virus right now from the world is a lot like trying to plan the construction of a stepping-stone pathway to the Moon. It's unrealistic," Michael Osterholm, an epidemiologist at the University of Minnesota in Minneapolis told the magazine *Nature* in February 2021. Osterholm, along with the vast majority of experts polled by *Nature*, predicted COVID-19 would become an endemic virus, which would "continue to circulate in pockets of the global population."[1]

I know this is true, and watching the case rates tick up yet again, the optimism I had in May and June feels a bit foolish now. But allowing yourself a dose of happiness, even a dose of delusion, is also very human. It's impossible to get up and parent and work every day without any hope for the future.

Two things have been my solace since March 2020, and they continue to bring me joy on days when I feel like planning for the future is an exercise in masochism. One is just being present with my children in ways I could not be before the pandemic, and I don't mean that in the "everyone just needs to meditate!" kind of way that always makes me furious. I mean truly being in their time, in little moments throughout the day that make me feel like I know them on a deeper level than I did before.

It means that now I know all my older daughter's favorite worlds in Roblox (Adopt Me and Brookhaven), and I know that she traded her flying cow to her friend Ella for a flying panda and regretted it. I know that my younger daughter likes to have solo dance parties in her room and that her greatest fear is never being able to do a cartwheel. While I knew these kinds of details about their lives before, the connection we have now feels more effortless. I feel so much more able to shed the bullshit messages about how a mother should be, and just *be* with my kids.

When I am happily ensconced with my children, I often think about this passage from Heidi Julavits's book *The Folded Clock: A Diary*:

> Today I spun tops with my son. We did this for six straight hours. So much of the pleasure of hanging out with children is successfully losing yourself, if only for a minute or two, in the activity with which you're both engaged. Suddenly, I am drawing a shoe that makes us both happy. The cogs of the day smoothly and quickly turn. Once I've finished the shoe, however, I am back to wondering—how can this day not mostly involve my waiting for it to be over? Yet when this day has ended my child will be older and I will be nearer to dead. Why should I wish for this to happen any sooner than it already will?[2]

The other thing that allows me to have hope is the remarkable moms I talk to every day for my job. The ones who are going through hell, and yet still put one foot in front of the other for their families. The ones who are making changes to their intimate relationships to better serve them. The ones who risked their lives to help others working outside the home during the pandemic and continue to do so even when they are profoundly demoralized.

The moms you'll meet in the first half of this chapter have been galvanized by the pandemic to make big changes in their communities even while managing their families through a crisis. Their work is remarkable and their spirit is contagious. After decades of work from so many politicians, activists, and writers, there finally seems to be some movement and support for policies that may help mothers and their families going forward, which you'll learn about in the second half of the chapter. And that gives me hope, too.

"EVERY DAY, I WAKE UP THINKING, 'WHAT CAN I DO FOR MY FAMILY?'"

Before 2020, Maebel Gebremedhin had barely done any community organizing. She is the mom of three boys, who are thirteen, seven, and three, and before the pandemic she was a music manager, running her ex-husband's career and booking shows. He's a successful music producer and DJ, and in the middle of March 2020, his work ground to a halt. He was about to get on a plane to do a show, and while he was packing, the show was canceled. "Everything had to shift, I had to find a new job," Maebel told me.

Everything changed again after George Floyd was murdered on May 25, 2020. "I felt very helpless. I felt there was not enough being done" to combat violence and racism against Black people, Maebel said. "I saw everyone taking to the streets, but children were left out of it. My three Black sons were affected by this, and it felt illogical" that they couldn't fully participate.

Maebel took her oldest son with her to protests in Brooklyn, where they live. He wanted to be seen and heard like everyone else, and they thought there should be a protest just for kids. In June 2020 in Brooklyn, "the protests were twenty-four hours a day, and the police were reacting very hard." Videos circulated of protesters getting rammed by an NYPD SUV.[3] "Families didn't feel like it was safe for their children, no matter how much they wanted to be part of it."

So Maebel decided to take action. First, she tried posting about organizing a children's march on her ex-husband's Instagram. He had over ten thousand followers, and just one person responded enthusiastically. "Out of ten thousand people! I thought more would come. So I started randomly reaching out to protest groups I had seen were in the New York area," she said.

She reached out to several, but only one wrote back to her, and they said, "'We love this idea, but we're really worried about doing this for children, we don't think it's safe.' I told them, 'Thanks for listening, I will continue. I will find other people who think this is something doable," Maebel said.

She continued asking people and drumming up enthusiasm, and finally the original organization she reached out to—a peaceful protest group called Warriors in the Garden—relented and helped her. They publicized the event on Instagram, and the Children's March ended up coming together in just a few days, with seven hundred parents and children gathering near Barclays Center in Brooklyn.[4]

"I was shocked by the amount of people that had come. It proved my point that families and children wanted to be involved," Maebel said. "This had been affecting every part of their lives, from waking up to going to sleep, the schools my children can go into, to zoning where we live. It felt really important for my boys to know their screaming was heard." Her then five-year-old made a speech that brought tears to her eyes. He said, wear a mask, I'm Black and I'm proud.

Maebel did not stop there. She created an organization called Moms Moving Forward[5] to organize other moms and create lasting change. She had to go back to work full time, which cut into the time she spent on activism, but then in early November 2020 she got more devastating news.

Maebel is from the Tigray region, a semiautonomous state in northern Ethiopia populated by ethnic Tigrayans, and most of her family is still there. That's when Prime Minister Abiy Ahmed began military action against the Tigray People's Liberation Front, a political party that's dominant in Tigray. Ahmed also cut off all telecommunication to the area.[6] Maebel could not reach her family and didn't know when she would be able to talk to them again.

The news that began to emerge from her homeland was horrific, and Maebel despaired. In early 2021, the *New York Times* would obtain an internal government report suggesting that tens of thousands of Tigrayans may have been killed. "Ethiopian officials and allied militia fighters are leading a systematic campaign of ethnic cleansing in Tigray, the war-torn region in northern Ethiopia," according to the report. "Whole villages were severely damaged or completely erased."[7] By August, bodies would be washing up on the shores of a river in nearby Sudan, and reports of massacres, famine, and sexual assault abounded.[8]

Maebel and her sister, Hawzien Gebremedhin, could not sit back and watch a genocide happen, and in January 2021 she put Moms Moving Forward aside and decided to start a nonprofit called the Tigray Action Committee[9] to raise awareness about the atrocities happening in Tigray, to petition the US government to impose sanctions on Ethiopia, and to raise money to send to the devastated region.

When I spoke to her in late July 2021, she said that what she had been able to accomplish in the past year was "incredible." They're doing press, and meeting with legislators to explain why it's important that what's happening in Tigray be labeled a genocide. But to her, it doesn't feel like enough "because our families are still in the midst of the genocide. Every day, I wake up thinking, 'What can I do for my family?' Just to bring it back to me as a parent, my boys are affected by this," she said.

Here in America, "My kids want for nothing. It doesn't matter how many jobs I have to take, if they want Starbucks every day? They will get it. You are wonderful, and I love you and it's not spoiling them in my mind. Then I think about their cousins literally starving [in Tigray]. We're hearing tomorrow is the last day food rations will last. I'm constantly juggling those two extremes."

Like Maebel, her sister didn't have any experience organizing a huge undertaking like this, and when I caught up with Maebel to fact-check in January 2022, they still had not been able to reach their family in Tigray. But they both feel an unending drive to save their family, and everyone else affected by the conflict. "I'm not who I was nine months ago, that was nothing," Maebel said. "It's just . . . I can't stop, I can't sleep." Yet she keeps going.[10]

INSPIRING THE NEXT GENERATION, THROUGH OSMOSIS AND LACK OF CHILDCARE

Before the pandemic, Sarah Stankorb adored her job as a nonpartisan elected official on the city council in Wyoming, Ohio, a suburb of Cincinnati. "I unreasonably love it. It's just Leslie Knope shooting out of me. It's so fun to be able to help people and see government in a way it can actually function," she said. It is basically a volunteer gig; she was paid around $5 a month, and at the beginning of 2020 she was in her second term on the council. The job was about ten hours a week then, and it dovetailed nicely with her freelance writing and taking care of her two kids, nine and twelve years old.

Her husband is a pediatric neurologist, and when life shut down in Ohio in March 2020, he was home for two months doing telemedicine. Whenever he was not seeing patients virtually in the basement, he parked himself at the dining room table, helping the kids with their schoolwork, while Sarah worked in her office. Even though their dad was right in front of them, whenever her kids had a question, they'd go and interrupt her instead. Many of her neighbors weren't taking the coronavirus as seriously as Sarah was, and were more relaxed in letting the kids get together at close range. Her son would cry to her about how hard it was to have the "mean mom," and it tore her apart to tell him, "I love you and I'm trying to keep you alive the best I know how."

Sarah also has a neurological condition called dystonia, which involves muscles contracting involuntarily, and it is exacerbated by stress. While the world was crumbling around her, her city council job filled all her free moments. Though they were getting guidance from the state, the city of Wyoming doesn't have its own health department, so the city council had to figure out what ordinances made sense for the health of their community. "I was doing too much, and constantly in the house with constant demands, and I was terrified that if I wasn't working my absolute hardest, the thing I wanted to do with my life"—writing—"I wouldn't be able to do," she said.

By the middle of 2020, Sarah's dystonia was worse than usual. As she wrote in a post on *Medium*:

Despite medication and quarterly Botox injections to quell my most overactive nerves, by the end of summer last year, the dystonia that twists my leg, spasms my shoulders, adds breaks to my voice, and jiggles my jaw manifested as an increasingly persistent head tremor too. My head was tremoring with a frequency that reflected how much stress had climbed into my nerves, balled up in the tissue those nerves activate, and it plucked, plucked away as anxiety weighed itself upon my shoulders. The world shut down, and yes-yes my head nodded. I feared my writing career would evaporate as my children and husband became fixtures in the rooms of our home where I spend my days working. *Yes-yes-yes* my head beat away. On our Zoom-streamed council meetings, when I took a sip of water, I had to use two hands to coordinate between twitchy arms and jerking head.[11]

Meanwhile, she was trying to seem as "stable and together" as she could. She was also trying to help the town navigate through fraught conversations about race and policing in the aftermath of George Floyd's murder. Part of what kept her going through this difficult period was seeing other moms in her community band together to create positive change. She mentioned a group called Wyoming Community in Action, which was founded by a group of community leaders who want to foster awareness around racial bias in their town. They put on a Juneteenth celebration in 2021, and continue to host discussions and events to further their mission.[12]

Despite the flaring of her condition, and the difficulty of the past year and a half, Sarah ran for and won her third term in November 2021, and was chosen by the city council to serve as vice mayor this term. But even before her recent win, Sarah knew she had already helped to make a difference in several ways.

As a person with a disability, she has championed disability rights in her community. When she learned from local parents that not one playground in her city was wheelchair accessible, she worked with families with children who had disabilities and, with the help of other city staff, ultimately got some state money to build a new universally accessible playground. The families also did private fundraising to get the project completed.

Sarah said it was a true group effort and that the meetings to figure out how to make it maximally accessible were the best she's ever had. Her working group of staff and community members invited kids with disabilities to give feedback on what kind of turf their wheelchairs might work best on, and what kind of playground equipment they could comfortably and enjoyably use.

Because Sarah had nowhere else to put her kids, they attended the meetings, too, even before the pandemic, and her son got involved "through osmosis and lack of childcare," she said. "I was looking for grants and my son was in Cub Scouts. As a service project, he started researching grant opportunities to pay for this playground. So he's learning how to help budget and fundraise."

Her daughter has also been inspired by Sarah's work on the city council. In her children's elementary school, they get a reward for good behavior, which is a sticker called "the caring cowboy." Both her kids thought there should be a caring cowgirl, too. Her son wrote a letter to the principal when he was in kindergarten, and then her daughter took it further. "My daughter got really interested in this sticker. She wrote a letter and requested a meeting with the principal." She organized a petition, formed a committee, and came to the meeting with an agenda. Her daughter even proposed a "caring cowkids" sticker "with lots of different types of kids," and although the sticker hasn't changed, "all these skills, these children have just absorbed all of this. That's the payout, I hope," she said.[13]

IMPARTING QUALITY INFORMATION IN A SEA OF NOISE

When Sheila Wijayasinghe entered lockdown, she was still on maternity leave from her job as a family doctor in Toronto. Her second child was four months old, and Sheila felt like "I was sort of watching from the sidelines. I felt guilty I wasn't there contributing" on the front lines of COVID-19.

Her area of interest and expertise has always been women's health and mental health. "During the pandemic especially, but always, women have carried this weight we don't really talk about enough." Sheila has experienced postpartum depression and went through fertility treatments to conceive her kids, and before the pandemic, she was able to share her experiences on a Canadian TV show called *The Social*, where she always got incredible feedback.

Because of Sheila's good experience sharing personal stories, a colleague reached out to her in April 2020. The quarantines meant that pregnant and postpartum women were not able to access their usual support systems—at that point their partners could not even come with them to medical appointments—and Sheila's colleague thought she could help start an Instagram account that would impart quality information in a sea of noise and misinformation.

So Sheila and a few coworkers at St. Michael's Hospital in Toronto started @pandemicpregnancyguide. Sheila thought they would have a hundred or so followers from their local patient population, but so many women across the world were hungry for accurate, evidence-based information on navigating pregnancy, birth, and newborn care during the pandemic that as of this writing they have over forty thousand followers.

But Sheila didn't stop there. When she went back to work in the fall of 2020, Toronto was experiencing a second wave of COVID-19, and the Pandemic Pregnancy Guide account was getting lots of panicked direct messages. These messages expressed anxiety about the virus, and also just deep sadness about the loss of typical new baby milestones. Questions like: When are the grandparents going to get to hold the baby?

Sheila remembered a children's book that had helped her through her fertility struggles, called *Wish*, which follows an elephant couple who long for a baby. It gave her hope when she felt hopeless. She wanted to give the same kind of relief to expectant parents and also hope that they could get through this hard time. So she partnered with an Italian illustrator named Anna Despina Koprantzelas to write a book called *Once Upon a Pandemic: A Pregnancy Journey*.[14]

The book provides a positive account of being pregnant during COVID-19. You can be pregnant in imperfect circumstances, the book encourages, and still find joy, love, and incredible meaning in your families.

Because one of Sheila's focus areas as a family doctor is intimate partner violence, the proceeds from *Once Upon a Pandemic* go to the Red Door Family Shelter, which provides emergency sanctuary to families fleeing from abuse, as well as to refugees and other folks experiencing homelessness. The United Nations calls violence against women during COVID-19 "the shadow pandemic," because "emerging data and reports from those on the front lines have shown that all types of violence against women and girls, particularly domestic violence, has intensified."[15] As Sheila put it, "Home is not always the safest place for people." I have heard from several off-the-record moms who had to initiate divorce proceedings during the pandemic due to abusive behavior from their partners that had intensified.

So far, Sheila has been able to donate thousands of dollars to the Red Door Family Shelter from sales of her book, and every printing she has run has sold out. Sheila said she also found writing the book to be a respite from the sad, hard work of her day job and from the stresses of parenting two young children. "It was a really good distraction," she said. "I came home from work, then I was full time on as a mom from five to eight, and then I had a space after that to do something that's personal and creative."[16]

HOW CAN WE FIX WHAT'S BROKEN?

If the pandemic has shed a light on anything, it is how absurd most of our historical expectations of women and motherhood are. It's also clear now to many more people that the expectations of ideal worker and ideal mother are in an unresolvable conflict, and that neither of those paradigms is good for our humanity or our happiness.

There were times when I was researching this book that I felt incredibly demoralized. In my own life, I worried about whether my kids were ever going to go back to school in any kind of normal way, whether they will be scarred for life, and whether I can keep working with them hanging around the house without completely disintegrating into a pile of fine dust swathed in unwashed athleisure.

Professionally, I spent many days listening to moms talk about how badly they had been treated in myriad ways and how it felt like society didn't care or value them, or their children. When I was reading books written in the past forty years, like *The Second Shift* and *The Managed Heart* by Arlie Russell Hochschild, *The Mommy Myth* by Susan Douglas and Meredith Michaels, and *The Price of Motherhood* by Ann Crittenden, in particular—it felt like societal change was glacial and near impossible.

I interviewed the historian Alice Kessler-Harris on one of those demoralizing days. I was carping about how it all felt a little hopeless, and I could see through the Zoom that she looked half exasperated and half amused; like she probably wanted to shake me a little for being such a short-sighted jerk. "From where I sit, probably your mother's generation, the changes have been enormous," she said.

She described how when she was pregnant with her first child, she was married to a man in medical school, and the other wives looked down on her because she was in graduate school. "They were horrified I wasn't having children fast enough or devoting myself to my husband's career," she said.[17] Then she paused, and added: "The changes have come from your generation."

Disregarding the motherhood ideals and advocating for changes to support mothers and their children is a tall order, and there is not a single change we can make that will be a panacea. The changes have to be multipronged—a combination of political shifts, workplace shifts, and interpersonal shifts. And I think we have reasons to be optimistic on all three fronts.

FIXING POLITICS

While there are a minority of loud voices like the rude comment-ers I mentioned in chapter 5 who gripe that children should be a personal responsibility and that parents who need help can go kick rocks, both childcare and paid leave are broadly popular political entitlements. Though the political wrangling to get them enacted seems, on some days, like an impossible barrier (I opened the paper in December 2021 to see West Virginia senator Joe Manchin deliv-ering a fatal blow to the Biden administration's Build Back Better plan of social services),[18] I try to be optimistic that we can get to a better place in my lifetime.

According to research from the First Five Years Fund, a non-profit group that advocates for high-quality early childcare edu-cation and care, 74 percent of all voters think that elected leaders "should make childcare and early learning a priority in 2021." Fur-thermore, 80 percent of all voters—93 percent of Democrats, 81 percent of independents, and 66 percent of Republicans—believe that there should be more federal funding to increase the number of childcare spots across the country. Tax credits to support parents and childcare facilities are also extremely popular across the political spectrum.[19]

Paid family leave, which briefly became a shimmering reality for many families during the pandemic as part of the Families First Coronavirus Response Act, evaporated on December 31, 2020.[20] But voters were not keen on it going away: According to multiple polls from the spring of 2021, over 80 percent of voters support paid family leave.[21] In Vox, Gregory Svirnovskiy argues that paid leave could be a major political issue in several 2022 Senate elections because it is so popular with independent voters, despite some hesitation from Republican leaders.

> To win a majority of the seven battleground seats up for grabs in 2022, Democrats and Republicans alike will need to appeal to the 20 percent of undecided voters across the states. [A poll from Global Strategy Group & Paid Leave for All Action suggests] undecided likely voters in the states surveyed lean slightly toward the Republican Party but become willing to support a generic Democrat candidate who supports paid leave by 46 percentage points.[22]

Let's not forget that five states have passed paid leave legislation since 2016, which means that nine states in total and Washington, DC, now offer paid leave for parents—suggesting the momentum is already there.[23] And during the pandemic, mothers of all political persuasions have made the case for more governmental support for parents. Abby McCloskey, the founder and principal of McCloskey Policy LLC, a research and consulting firm, who was policy director for Rick Perry's 2016 and Howard Schultz's 2020 presidential campaigns, wrote a piece for Politico in June 2021 called "Conservative Values Support Investing in Childcare as Infrastructure. Here's Why."[24]

In her article, McCloskey argues that parents spending high-quality time with their infants is widely accepted by all child development experts as better for babies' health and well-being, and that family values have long been a pillar of Republican values. And yet many mothers are pushed back into the workforce before their bodies have even recovered from childbirth, and many fathers can't even take a single day off to welcome a new child into their life.

When I spoke to McCloskey in the summer of 2021, she said, "I wrote the Politico piece because I think these are really important issues that need to be addressed, and if Republicans keep saying no, we're going to get the policy liberals want. We need to start putting forward ideas of our own. These are some of the biggest issues facing American families, and we should go on the offensive to talk about it." Her hope is to ultimately have workable bipartisan solutions that are sustainable, rather than permanently warring liberal and conservative ideas that get nothing done for parents.

She thinks the pandemic made it clear to many more leaders that our current system of zero paid leave isn't working. "More people are talking about it than they were before," McCloskey said, but "there's a lot of trip wires when you're talking about it, in terms of values and gender roles, that keeps the conversation really halted."

And yet McCloskey is optimistic about the prospect of forward motion on greater social and financial support for parents. "I am really hopeful because of the polling, and because of the demographic realities, that there will be changes made to benefit American families. Whether it's paid leave or childcare support, the status quo is increasingly untenable and that is recognized. The political parties that agree on nothing are both putting forth policies to help families with young children in particular," she said,[25] citing Utah senator Mitt Romney's 2021 Family Security Act, which proposed a universal child allowance.[26]

According to the Center for American Progress, a liberal think tank, this kind of plan could benefit a much broader range of families than are currently being served by the Child Tax Credit, which reduces tax liabilities for some parents. "Crucially, the Family Security Act is not dependent on earnings, meaning that unlike the existing Child Tax Credit, families with little or no federal income tax liability, who are often experiencing the worst poverty, would benefit."[27]

Still, the expansion of the Child Tax Credit, which reached the poorest families and went into effect for the year 2021, helped the poorest families. Though it did not get renewed in 2022, many hope it will someday become part of a more permanent solution. Chabeli Carrazana, an economy reporter for The 19th*, talked to moms across the country who felt that an ongoing Child Tax Credit would be a way for their families to claw their way out of poverty.

As an Arizona mom named Lori Ament told Carrazana, "I have this new monthly allotment to make sure that the health and well-being of my family is provided for . . . More than making sure that I can afford daycare for my kid, which is a huge factor, or putting food on the table, which is a huge factor, I also see it as a mental well-being of both the parents and the child."[28]

Reshma Saujani ran for Congress as a Democrat in 2010 and, after visiting schools and seeing the gender gap in children's computer classes, founded the nonprofit organization Girls Who Code, which seeks to increase the number of women in computer science jobs. Right before the pandemic hit, she was in a wonderful spot: Her second child was born to a surrogate, after she had struggled for years with "horrible" infertility. Girls Who Code had its first Super Bowl ad, and the organization had never been in a better spot.

By March 15, 2020, everything had come crashing down, and suddenly she was homeschooling her older child and trying to save her nonprofit, which was rapidly losing sponsors as people made cutbacks to weather the uncertain times ahead. "I was working more hours than I could count. My liver failed, I had acne. I got Covid and it barely registered," Saujani told me. As she helped her child through remote pre-K, "every mom on the Zoom screen looked exactly like I felt."

When September rolled around in New York, where she lives, most children were still not back to school full time. She and most of her leadership team were moms of young children, and they were all barely holding it together. Then in December, there was an abysmal jobs report from the Bureau of Labor Statistics: "All of the Jobs Lost in December Were Women's Jobs," the National Women's Law Center announced. "There were nearly 2.1 million fewer women in the labor force in December than there were in February, before the pandemic started."[29]

Saujani had had enough. "I write best when I'm angry," she said. She wrote an op-ed for the *Hill*, calling for "a Marshall Plan for Moms," a federal task force dedicated to safely reopening schools, and that also "includes a monthly, means-tested $2,400 monthly payment to the women who are the bedrock of our economy and our society."[30] What ended up in the op-ed "was what my PTA moms and I were talking about. Every mom I knew needed cash, to figure out whether she had to pay the rent or get a tutor or buy some shoes for her kids. It was critical for her. A lack of cash might mean she has to go work the night shift, or go on food stamps."

She knows how important affordable childcare is because she didn't have it as a kid. Her parents were refugees, and she was a latchkey kid from the time she started elementary school. After her op-ed got so much attention, she made the Marshall Plan for Moms into an ongoing campaign, one that includes lobbying for policies like paid family leave, affordable childcare, and pay equity.

Her comments around paid leave and childcare were not dissimilar to Abby McCloskey's, which is heartening. "In this moment, as the country is so sick and tired of people not being able to get together and get things done, motherhood is a bipartisan issue," Saujani said. "We can get people together around supporting moms. I believe that, and the data shows that."[31]

FIXING WORK

Paid leave and help with childcare will go a long way to help mothers. But this problem needs help from workplaces, too. The American way of work isn't just crushing parents; it's unsustainable for everyone.

We work longer hours than comparable industrialized countries, but have far less of a safety net because we have no nationalized health care and no federal sick leave policy. As Derek Thompson explains in the *Atlantic*, "No large country in the world as productive as the United States averages more hours of work a year. And the gap between the U.S. and other countries is growing. Between 1950 and 2012, annual hours worked per employee fell by about 40 percent in Germany and the Netherlands—but by only 10 percent in the United States."[32]

Millennials are suffering in particular from excess work, mostly because my generation has nothing to show for it. We are drowning in student debt (about $500 billion of it),[33] and we have already experienced two major recessions in our adult lives—the great recession and financial crisis of 2008, and the pandemic—both of which made even the wealthiest and best-educated Americans afraid of losing their jobs.

It's all pretty gnarly for us, according to the *Wall Street Journal*: "The economic hit of the coronavirus pandemic is emerging as particularly bad for millennials, born between 1981 and 1996, who as a group hadn't recovered from the experience of entering the workforce during the previous financial crisis. For this cohort, already indebted and a step behind on the career ladder, this second pummeling could keep them from accruing the wealth of older generations."[34] The notion that we could work such long hours for our entire lives and still be in precarious circumstances when we try to retire is existentially exhausting. No wonder the writer Anne Helen Petersen dubbed millennials "the burnout generation."

While our workplaces can't guarantee us stability in an ever-changing world, they can vastly improve our experiences. The first thing workplaces can do is put in place paid caregiving leave policies for all workers. If paid family leave is only associated with mothers, women will continue to be seen as lesser employees: the motherhood penalty will continue.

When paid leave is only for parents, it also leaves out the millions of workers who need time off to care for older or sick loved ones. According to a 2020 report from the AARP Public Policy Institute, nearly thirty million Americans "are caring for an ill friend or family member while also working at a paying job," which is an increase of around 5 million since 2015.[35] This caretaking affects work performance in the same way childcare breakdowns affect work performance. As the AARP report notes, "Over half (53 percent) say they have to go in late, leave early, or take time off to provide care. Fifteen percent reported reducing their hours, 14 percent took leave and many reported receiving warnings about their performance or attendance, turning down a promotion, quitting, retiring or losing benefits." Providing paid caretaking leave for everyone may also lessen the bitterness some child-free employees feel about what they consider unfair benefits that parents receive.

Taking leave must be modeled from the top down to make it stick. White-collar workers take their cues from upper management, and if there is a leave policy on the books but the executive suite never misses a day, you can bet that the rest of the company is going to take that as a tacit acknowledgment that caretaking leave isn't actually acceptable. As Nathaniel Popper pointed out in 2019, "Some studies do show that taking paternity leave can damage a man's professional reputation and affect his future earning potential."[36] Let's not let that continue: the more people who take parental leave, the better for all.

The other major way we can make work more friendly to caregivers is to give people more control over their lives. One fix is to give workers more advance notice of those schedules. As noted earlier, "just in time" scheduling means 20 percent of workers don't know their work hours until a week or less in advance. Wrangling care last minute is extremely difficult, and low-wage workers can't afford to pay for care they're not using.

Some companies are listening to caregivers and making repairs to their corporate culture in the aftermath of COVID-19. As the *New York Times'* gender reporter Alisha Haridasani Gupta pointed out, in August 2021:

> Executives from nearly two hundred companies, including JPMorgan Chase, Patagonia and Spotify, acknowledged that the caregiving crisis was affecting their operations—and ultimately their bottom lines—and that they needed to craft workplace policies that would better support caregivers in the long run. What might that look like? Potentially a lot more flexibility. Shorter workweeks and greater control over work hours, free or subsidized on-site or center-based childcare facilities and expanded paid parental leave—policies for which advocates, grass-roots organizations and voters from both sides of the aisle have long been clamoring.[37]

It is now becoming clearer to some employers what's been obvious to moms for decades: that without childcare and schools, we cannot have a functioning economic system.

FIXING THE CULTURE

Altering our interpersonal dynamics might be the most difficult fix of all. "I think cultural change is the most important piece, but also the hardest part," said Reshma Saujani. "I think it's the hardest part because so much of what it means to be a mom is so baked into America." As the cliché goes, "Mom" is as American as apple pie, and I have outlined all the ways in which the cultural ideals of the selfless, immaculate mother who sacrifices her whole person to her child has roots that are centuries old.

While the ideals may always exist in some form, more and more of us can reject them. As individuals, we can surround ourselves with people who support and affirm our values, rather than tear us down. We aren't all going to have the same parenting styles, and we're not all going to have the same personal or work goals, and that is how it should be.

There are a multitude of ways to raise thriving children because children are their own little people. One of the great joys of motherhood, for me, has been learning from my kids who they are and what they need; even within a single family, each child will have her own desires, dreams, and preferences. Anyone who tries to tell you there's just one way to parent every single child—and it's *their* way—is toxic. We can accept, as mothers, that we can't control every outcome for our children. If COVID-19 has taught us anything, it's that we ultimately cannot keep our children safe from every problem, every ill. There is too much that is out of our hands, and all we can do is love our children and send them off into the world.

Every family has its own cultural traditions and rules, and those should be honored and appreciated, too. We pretend that the Donna Reed life is still the norm, but in fact, fewer than half of children under eighteen live with two married, heterosexual parents in their first marriage, and 41 percent of children are born to unmarried parents.[38] In 1960, 73 percent of children lived with two married hetero parents in their first marriage.[39] Times have changed, and instead of trying to go backward, the culture needs to catch up.

It's not realistic to say we'll never judge each other. But we can do our best to keep our judgments off the internet and out of the public square because in our hearts we know that almost all parents are just trying to do their best.

If we have partners, we can speak honestly about how to make things feel fair. That doesn't necessarily mean cutting every bit of domestic responsibility absolutely down the center because that's not realistic for most families. It means being *real* partners and working together, especially through the difficult early years of parenting. Part of that work means sometimes training the outside world to realize that Mom does not have to be the go-to. Over the years, the couples I have talked to who have the most egalitarian relationships, like Myra Jones-Taylor, go out of their way to put the father's name and number on forms, and to cc both partners on emails concerning the children. The dentist's office may keep calling Mom to schedule appointments, so sometimes Dad needs to be proactive and make it clear that he's the point of contact.

Changing the culture also means putting in work to improve our communities, the way Maebel Gebremedhin, Sarah Stankorb, and Sheila Wijayasinghe are working close to home and around the world. Helping our communities doesn't necessarily mean you need to start a nonprofit or run for office.

It can mean watching your neighbor's kids when they're in a pinch, donating to your local diaper bank, or attending school board meetings. We also need to acknowledge that different communities need different solutions. What parents need where I live in Brooklyn, an expensive major urban center with public transportation, is going to be very different from what parents need in rural Idaho.

I asked many of the historians, sociologists, and policy experts I spoke to for this book why they thought progress had stalled when it comes to mothers. The comment that came up over and over again was that America wears moms out to the point that we are just too exhausted to agitate for the changes we need to make our lives better.

As Katha Pollitt put it in a 2019 *New York Times* op-ed arguing for universal day care, which had been curiously absent from the progressive agenda pre-pandemic:

Maybe the newly radicalized young haven't had kids yet. For them, student debt is a more immediate problem. And maybe parents are just too tired to fight for it when they need it, and then the kids are in school and they don't need it anymore. The childcare crunch is a bit like childbirth. Once it's over, it's over, and you're in a new place in your life. And in that new place it's easy to forget how expensive and frustrating the quest for good reliable childcare was, and for women to rationalize lost opportunities and less equality at home as just some of the many trade-offs motherhood involves.[40]

We have never been more exhausted than we are now because of all the stressors brought on by the pandemic, and we can't do it all alone. We are burned out and we feel betrayed by an unfeeling culture. But we owe it to the next generation of mothers to keep advocating for changes that might not benefit our families in the near term. And we owe it to our future selves to make our own lives more equal. If we don't start working on it now, we will be mothering the whole world—at home and at work—for the rest of our lives.

We need allies in our lives, in our workplaces, and in our government who are going to use their power to make the United States a friendlier place for our families. Our health, and the health of generations to come, depends on it.

Conclusion

I met up with a friend in January 2022 for coffee and a walk. I hadn't seen her in person for years, since we both had young kids at home and the pandemic made meeting up impossible. As she turned toward me, I saw an undeniable bump under her snug jacket.

As we began our stroll around the neighborhood she started talking about how she wasn't feeling excited about having another baby. Though she theoretically wanted another—this kid wasn't an oops—she was exhausted from working and parenting her first child. In our conversation, I gently Pollyanna'd her. I did not even realize I was doing it, but I kept parrying her ambivalence with positivity: Once the baby is here, you'll feel better! Babies are so cute and snuggly! Part of me wishes I had another!

She said something like: I think a lot of people are freaked out by my ambivalence, but it's where I am right now.

I apologized and just listened. And as she spoke, I realized that accepting and sitting with ambivalence, our own and other mothers', might be the most essential takeaway from this book. I couldn't believe that after spending years researching and writing about moms and the unreasonable pressures on us, my knee-jerk reaction to an honest conversation was to push it away. I felt awful that I was still conditioned to slap a happy face on her mixed feelings—who wouldn't feel ambivalent about having a newborn in the middle of a pandemic?

We can advocate for better policies in our workplaces and government, and we can vote for politicians who support parents. But it's obvious that major systemic change is going to take years, if not decades, to implement, and American mothers need help right now. As individuals, what we can do today, and every day moving forward, is allow ourselves and other moms to be fully human. Because there is something deeply dehumanizing about constantly being told to erase parts of yourself.

One of the most damaging parts of the American motherhood ideal is that we aren't supposed to express anything but perfect love for our children. No one feels perfect love for anything all the time, and it doesn't make you a bad mother or a bad person to admit that out loud. I often think of a piece of advice from my own mother, who is both wise and practiced psychiatry for forty years: Even about the things we love most, we are truly ambivalent.

Ambivalence, in psychoanalytic terms, is not indifference or mixed feelings, as the late psychotherapist Rozsika Parker explained in her book *Torn in Two: The Experience of Maternal Ambivalence*. Ambivalence means "quite contradictory impulses and emotions towards the same person co-exist. The positive and negative components sit side by side and remain in opposition."[1] We will feel strong pulls of adoration and rage and every emotion in between. Parker described maternal ambivalence as "normal, natural and eternal."

The eternal part of ambivalence is key. Sometimes we imagine mothers of the past as more essentially maternal in some way, as if modern life has stripped away the pure joys of motherhood. But when you read women's diaries and letters from the past three hundred years, as I have done while researching this book, that could not be further from the truth.

In *Scarlett's Sisters: Young Women in the Old South*, the historian Anya Jabour collected so many incredible, honest sentiments from mothers of the nineteenth century. These women described giving birth as a "dreaded ordeal," and a "constant & never ceasing horror" in their diaries and letters. The mother of a sleepless, colicky infant wrote of the "hard feelings" she had toward her baby son. "I fear I am not very charitable towards babies . . . as I find myself at such times wishing for 'a lodge in some vast wilderness, where the cry of babies might never reach me more.'" Another woman said the thought of nursing her baby for the rest of her life made her want to "lie down & die."[2]

They also write of the unexpected pleasures of motherhood—"*Baby walks*, actually trots all over the room by herself—is it not delightful?" And when these young women would write to their closest female family and friends, they were looking for solace, connection, and understanding, to feel their joys and their disappointments without judgment. It's still what many of us are looking for when we share our truths, whatever they might be, with the ones we love and trust the most.

The guilt we feel for having all the feelings is compounding our eternal exhaustion. The fear we have of being found out as less than perfect mothers keeps us from being truly honest.

If we could stop layering guilt atop ourselves every single day, what could we accomplish? What might become clear about our own values? What could we have the energy and will to fight for, if we were less concerned about how "bad" we are?

I know it's easier said than done. We can't just shed several lifetimes of cultural conditioning in one fluid motion. But we can start by listening to ourselves.

Acknowledgments

I'd like to start by thanking my agent, Elisabeth Weed, and my editor, Kate Nintzel, both of whom have been tireless supporters of me and my work for over a decade. They saw countless versions of this book in proposal form over the years, and they kept pushing me to move forward with it. The book would not exist without both of them cheering me on. I would also like to thank everyone at Harper-Collins, Mariner, and The Book Group who contributed to getting this book to the finish line, including Molly Gendell, David Wienir, Brettne Bloom, Laura Brady, and so many others.

Thank you to Hilary McClellen, whose fantastic attention to detail and fact-checking prowess saved me in so many ways.

Thank you to every person who spoke to me for this book—it was an honor to hear your stories and your expertise.

So many of my friends and colleagues read chapters of this book, gave me advice, referred me to sources, or offered words of encouragement during the worst parts of the pandemic when they surely had better things to do. Thank you to Leah Chernikoff, Laia Garcia,

Kaitlyn Greenidge, Jessica Winter, Emily Gould, Jessica Pressler, Emma Straub, Jackie Thomas-Kennedy, Johanna Cox, Sally Law Errico, Anne Helen Petersen, Charlie Warzel, Jason Zinoman, The Splinters, Elizabeth Greenwood, David Plotz, Noreen Malone, Angela Garbes, Dixa Ramirez, Heather Havrilesky, Emilie Spiegel, Hanna Rosin, and Emily Bazelon.

My coworkers and pals at the *Times* provided so much practical support and wise counsel. I am grateful every day to have the best job in the business. Thank you to Monica Drake, Katie Kingsbury, Farah Miller, Melonyce McAfee, David Yee, Natalie Raimondi, Jessica Bennett, Lindsey Underwood, Heather Murphy, Caitlin Roper, Dani Blum, David Swerdlick, Brian Zittel, Jia Lynn Yang, Lori Leibovich, and Sam Sifton.

Books do not get written by parents during the pandemic without the care of their village. Thank you to all the people who took care of my kids and me since 2020: Shelly Alcindor, Annie Rauwerda, Jenny Woodson, Devin Cain, Roy Cox, Misty Cox, Thornton McEnery, and Kristen Crofoot.

I have always been grateful for having such an unconditionally loving and supportive family whose company I cherish. The pandemic made me even more full of adoration and appreciation for: David, Charlotte, Wendell, Noah, Jud, Meghan, Jacob, Anna, Penny, Mary, Chase, Mark, Lucy, Bryan, all the other aunts, uncles, and cousins, and my nieces and nephews.

I am beyond thankful for my mom and dad, Judith and Richard. Living with them during parts of 2020 and 2021 brought some of the greatest, unexpected joys of my adult life. We would have fallen apart without you there, and my kids are so lucky to have such wonderful grandparents living nearby.

If all husbands were like Mike, I would not have had to write this book. He's such an excellent dad and partner. Thanks for putting up with the mood pockets and gremlin states required to write this book over the past two years. I love you.

To my two girls, this book is ultimately for you. Becoming your mom was the best thing I ever did. I hope that by the time you are grown-ups, and maybe mothers yourselves, the world is a better place for you.

Notes

INTRODUCTION

1. Sheryl Sandberg, "Why We Have Too Few Women Leaders," TED-Women2010, December 2010, https://www.ted.com/talks/sheryl_sandberg _why_we_have_too_few_women_leaders.
2. "What Is the Risk for Relapse after Stopping Antidepressants During Pregnancy?" MGH Center for Women's Mental Health, July 1, 2020, https:// womensmentalhealth.org/posts/discontinuation/.
3. Family and Medical Leave Act, U.S Department of Labor, accessed December 5, 2021, https://www.dol.gov/sites/dolgov/files/WHD/legacy/files/whdfs 28.pdf.
4. Julia M. Goodman, Holly Elser, and William H. Dow, "Among Low-Income Women in San Francisco, Low Awareness of Paid Parental Leave Benefits Inhibits Take-Up," *Health Affairs* 39, no. 7 (July 2020), https://www.health affairs.org/doi/10.1377/hlthaff.2020.00157.
5. Interview with Patrice Gamble, June 25, 2021.
6. Matt Barnum, "Parents Are Spending New Child Benefit on Food, Education. But Will Congress Keep It?" *Chalkbeat*, November 21, 2021, https:// www.chalkbeat.org/2021/11/15/22783579/child-tax-credit-schools-biden -reconciliation-plan-education-poverty-families-research.
7. Alicia Adamczyk, "Parents Can No Longer Count on Monthly Child Tax Credit Payments," CNBC, January 7, 2022, https://www.cnbc. com/2022/01/07/parents-can-no-longer-count-on-monthly-child-tax-credit -payments.html.

CHAPTER 1: HOW DID WE GET HERE?

1. Irene Oh, "Motherhood in Christianity and Islam: Critiques, Realities, and Possibilities," *Journal of Religious Ethics* 38, no. 4 (December 2010): 638–53.

2. Agnes R. Howard, *Showing What Pregnancy Tells Us about Being Human* (Eerdmans, 2020).

3. Mary E. Fissell, "Hairy Women and Naked Truths: Gender and the Politics of Knowledge in 'Aristotle's Masterpiece,'" *William and Mary Quarterly* 60, no. 1 (Jan. 2003): 43–74, https://www.jstor.org/stable/3491495.

4. Jacqueline Jones, *American Work: Four Centuries of Black and White Labor* (W. W. Norton & Company, 1998), p. 39.

5. Jones, *American Work*, chap. 1.

6. Mary Beth Norton, "The Evolution of White Women's Experience in Early America," *American Historical Review* 89, no. 3 (June 1984): 593–619, https://www.jstor.org/stable/1856118.

7. Norton, "The Evolution of White Women's Experience."

8. Norton, "The Evolution of White Women's Experience."

9. Jodi Vandenberg-Daves, *Modern Motherhood: An American History*, https://www.jstor.org/stable/j.ctt6wqb20.5.

10. Nancy Schrom Dye and Daniel Blake Smith, "Mother Love and Infant Death, 1750–1920," *Journal of American History* 73, no. 2 (Sept. 1986): 329–53.

11. Ruth H. Bloch, "American Feminine Ideals in Transition: The Rise of the Moral Mother, 1785–1815," *Feminist Studies* 4, no. 2, Toward a Feminist Theory of Motherhood (June 1978), pp. 100–26, https://www.jstor.org/stable/3177453.

12. Hugh Cunningham, *Children and Childhood in Western Society Since 1500* (Routledge; 2nd edition, 2005).

13. Lawrence Stone, *The Family, Sex and Marriage in England 1500–1800* (Harper Perennial, 1977), p. 150.

14. Nancy F. Cott, *The Bonds of Womanhood: "Woman's Sphere" in New England, 1780–1835* (Yale University Press, second edition 1997).

15. Stephanie Coontz, *Marriage, a History: How Love Conquered Marriage* (Penguin Books, 2005), p. 146.

16. Coontz, *Marriage, a History*, p. 146.

17. Coontz, *Marriage, a History*, p. 156.

18. Sharon Hays, *The Cultural Contradictions of Motherhood* (Yale University Press, 1996), p. 35.

19. Dorothy Roberts, *Killing the Black Body: Race, Reproduction, and the Meaning of Liberty* (Vintage, 1997), pp. 77–78.

20. Linda Kerber, "The Republican Mother: Women and the Enlightenment—An American Perspective," *American Quarterly* 28, no. 2, Special Issue: An American Enlightenment (Summer 1976): 187–205, https://www.jstor.org/stable/2712349.

21. Kerber, "The Republican Mother."

22. For example, through a loophole that did not explicitly bar women from voting, there was female suffrage in the state of New Jersey from 1776 to 1807, but that loophole was ultimately closed. From: Judith Apter Klinghoffer

and Lois Elkis, "'The Petticoat Electors': Women's Suffrage in New Jersey, 1776–1807," *Journal of the Early Republic* 12, no. 2 (Summer 1992): 159–93, https://www.jstor.org/stable/3124150.

23. "H. R. 40, Naturalization Bill, March 4, 1790," Records of the U.S. Senate, National Archives and Records Administration, accessed on June 20, 2021, https://www.visitthecapitol.gov/exhibitions/artifact/h-r-40-naturalization-bill -march-4-1790.

24. "H. R. 40, Naturalization Bill."

25. Marilyn S. Blackwell, "The Republican Vision of Mary Palmer Tyler," from *Mothers and Motherhood: Readings in American History,* edited by Rima D. Apple and Janet Golden (Ohio State University Press, 1997), p. 36.

26. Blackwell, "The Republican Vision," p. 31.

27. Catharine A. Beecher, "An Address on Female Suffrage," speech delivered in the Music Hall of Boston, 1870, https://www.gutenberg.org /files/56090/56090-h/56090-h.htm#An_Address_on_Female_Suffrage.

28. Catharine A. Beecher, *A Treatise on Domestic Economy: For the Use of Young Ladies at Home and at School* (Harper & Brothers, 1845), accessed from Project Gutenberg, https://www.gutenberg.org/files/21829/21829 -h/21829-h.htm.

29. Katy Simpson Smith, *We Have Raised All of You: Motherhood in the South, 1750–1835* (Louisiana State University Press, 2013), p. 83.

30. Simpson Smith, *We Have Raised All of You*, p. 83.

31. Interview with Anya Jabour, October 20, 2020.

32. Jennifer Medina, Katie Benner, and Kate Taylor, "Actresses, Business Leaders and Other Wealthy Parents Charged in U.S. College Entry Fraud," *New York Times,* March 12, 2019, https://www.nytimes.com/2019/03/12/us/college -admissions-cheating-scandal.html.

33. Simpson Smith, *We Have Raised All of You*, p. 95.

34. Simpson Smith, *We Have Raised All of You*, p. 95.

35. Simpson Smith, *We Have Raised All of You*, p. 96.

36. Anna Glasier et al., "Contraception After Pregnancy," *Acta Obstetricia et Gynecologica Scandinavica* (Nov. 2019), https://pubmed.ncbi.nlm.nih .gov/31001809/.

37. Judith Walzer Leavitt, "'Science' Enters the Birthing Room: Obstetrics in America since the Eighteenth Century," *Journal of American History* 70, no. 2 (Sept. 1983): 281–304.

38. M Cobb, "An Amazing 10 Years: The Discovery of Egg and Sperm in the 17th Century," *Reproduction in Domestic Animals* 47 (Suppl. 4, 2012): 2–6, https://onlinelibrary.wiley.com/doi/pdf/10.1111/j.1439-0531.2012.02105.x.

39. Interview with Shannon Withycombe, assistant professor of history at the University of New Mexico, September 22, 2020.

40. Matthew L. Edwards and Anwar D. Jackson, "The Historical Development of Obstetric Anesthesia and Its Contributions to Perinatology," *American Journal of Perinatology* (Feb. 2016): 211–16.

41.   Walzer Leavitt, "'Science' Enters the Birthing Room," pp. 281–304.
42.   Walzer Leavitt, "'Science' Enters the Birthing Room," pp. 281–304.
43.   Walzer Leavitt, "'Science' Enters the Birthing Room," pp. 281–304.
44.   Carroll Smith-Rosenberg and Charles Rosenberg, "The Female Animal: Medical and Biological Views of Woman and Her Role in Nineteenth-Century America," *Journal of American History* 60, no. 2 (Sept. 1973): 332–56.
45.   Interview with Withycombe.
46.   Interview with Withycombe.
47.   Alice Kessler-Harris, *Out to Work: A History of Wage-Earning Women in the United States* (Oxford University Press; 20th edition, 2003), p. 46.
48.   Interview with Alice Kessler-Harris, July 1, 2021.
49.   Interview with Kessler-Harris, p. 49.
50.   Interview with Kessler-Harris, p. 55.
51.   Interview with Kessler-Harris, pp. 80–81.
52.   Interview with Kessler-Harris, p. 51.
53.   Grace H. Dodge, Thomas Hunter, et al., *What Women Can Earn: Occupations of Women and Their Compensation* (F. A. Stokes, 1899).
54.   Dodge et al., *What Women Can Earn*, pp. 229–30.
55.   Coontz, *Marriage, a History*, p. 186.
56.   Anya Jabour, *Scarlett's Sisters: Young Women in the Old South* (University of North Carolina Press, 2007).
57.   Rima D. Apple, "Constructing Mothers: Scientific Motherhood in the Nineteenth and Twentieth Centuries," *Social History of Medicine* 8, no. 2 (August 1995): 161–78.
58.   Torborg Lundell, "Ellen Key and Swedish Feminist Views on Motherhood," *Scandinavian Studies* 56, no. 4 (Autumn, 1984): 351–69.
59.   Ellen Key, *The Century of the Child* (G. P. Putnam's Sons, 1909), p. 72.
60.   Key, *The Century of the Child*, p. 102.
61.   Children's Bureau, US Department of Health & Human Services, *The Children's Bureau Legacy: Ensuring the Right to Childhood*.
62.   *Children's Bureau Legacy*.
63.   Regina Markell Morantz, "Making Women Modern: Middle Class Women and Health Reform in 19th Century America," *Journal of Social History* 10, no. 4 (Summer 1977): 490–507.
64.   *Children's Bureau Legacy*.
65.   Mrs. Max West, "Prenatal Care," Care of Children Series, no. 1, Bureau Publications no. 4, Government Printing Office, 1913.
66.   Nancy Woloch, *A Class by Herself: Protective Laws for Women Workers, 1890s–1990s* (Princeton University Press, 2015): 6–7, https://www.jstor.org/stable/j.ctt1h4mhr9.4.
67.   Woloch, *Class by Herself*, p. 22.
68.   Woloch, *Class by Herself*, p. 75.
69.   "*Curt Muller, Plff. in Err., v. State of Oregon*," Legal Information Institute,

Cornell Law School, accessed on July 3, 2021, https://www.law.cornell.edu/supremecourt/text/208/412.

70. Alice Kessler-Harris, *Women Have Always Worked: A Concise History* (University of Illinois Press, 2018), p. 123.

71. Virginia MacMakin Collier, *Marriage and Careers: A Study of One Hundred Women Who Are Wives, Mothers, Homemakers and Professional Workers* (Channel Bookshop, 1926).

72. Collier, *Marriage and Careers*, p. 18.

73. Collier, *Marriage and Careers*, p. 18.

74. Collier, *Marriage and Careers*, pp. 68–69.

75. Ann Crittenden, *The Price of Motherhood: Why the Most Important Job in the World Is Still the Least Valued* (Picador, 10th anniversary edition, 2001, 2010), p. 65.

76. Crittenden, *Price of Motherhood*, p. 65.

77. Roberts, *Killing the Black Body*, p. 291.

78. US Department of Labor, *Wage and Hour Division*, accessed July 5, 2021, https://www.dol.gov/agencies/whd/about/history.

79. Woloch, *Class by Herself*, pp. 164–65.

80. Betsey Stevenson, "An 'Experiment' in Universal Child Care in the United States: Lessons from the Lanham Act," White House (blog post), January 22, 2015, https://obamawhitehouse.archives.gov/blog/2015/01/22/experiment-universal-child-care-united-states-lessons-lanham-act.

81. Lydia Kiesling, "Paid Child Care for Working Mothers? All It Took Was a World War," *New York Times,* October 2, 2019, https://www.nytimes.com/2019/10/02/us/paid-childcare-working-mothers-wwii.html.

82. CDC, "Achievements in Public Health, 1900–1999: Healthier Mothers and Babies," *Morbidity and Mortality Weekly Report* 48, no. 38 (Oct. 1, 1999): 849–58, https://www.cdc.gov/mmwr/preview/mmwrhtml/mm4838a2.htm.

83. CDC, "Achievements in Public Health, 1900–1999."

84. Ephrat Livni and Dan Kopf, "The Decline of the Large US Family, in Charts," *Quartz,* October 11, 2017, https://qz.com/1099800/average-size-of-a-us-family-from-1850-to-the-present/.

85. Rima D. Apple, *Perfect Motherhood: Science and Childrearing in America* (Rutgers University Press, 2006), p. 74.

86. Jonathan Metzl, "'Mother's Little Helper': The Crisis of Psychoanalysis and the Miltown Resolution," *Gender & History* 15 no. 2 (August 2003): 240–67.

87. Ziv Eisenberg, "Clear and Pregnant Danger: The Making of Prenatal Psychology in Mid-Twentieth-Century America," *Journal of Women's History* 22, no. 3 (Fall 2010): 112–35.

88. Eisenberg, "Clear and Pregnant Danger."

89. Eisenberg, "Clear and Pregnant Danger."

90. Anne Harrington, "Mother Love and Mental Illness: An Emotional History," *Osiris* 31, no. 1 (2016), https://www.journals.uchicago.edu/doi/full/10.1086/687559.

91. Harrington, "Mother Love and Mental Illness."

92. Jordynn Jack, *Autism and Gender: From Refrigerator Mothers to Computer Geeks* (University of Illinois Press, 2014), p. 33, https://www.jstor.org/stable/pdf/10.5406/j.ctt7zw5k5.5.pdf.

93. Trude Tietze, "A Study of Mothers of Schizophrenic Patients," *Interpersonal and Biological Processes* 12 (1949).

94. Jack, *Autism and Gender,* p. 35.

95. Edward Dolnick, *Madness on the Couch: Blaming the Victim in the Heyday of Psychoanalysis* (Simon & Schuster, 2007).

96. Ben Wattenberg, "Working Women," *The First Measured Century*, PBS, accessed July 4, 2021, https://www.pbs.org/fmc/book/2work8.htm.

97. Apple, *Perfect Motherhood*, p. 111.

98. Kessler-Harris, *Out to Work,* p. 312.

99. Stephanie Coontz, *The Way We Never Were: American Families and the Nostalgia Trap* (Basic Books, 1993), 41.

100. Adrienne Rich, *Of Woman Born: Motherhood as Experience and Institution* (W. W. Norton & Company, 1986), p. 24.

101. Stephanie Coontz, *A Strange Stirring: The Feminine Mystique and American Women at the Dawn of the 1960s* (Basic Books, 2011), p. 4.

102. National Organization for Women, "Founding," accessed April 11, 2021, https://now.org/about/history/founding-2/.

103. US Equal Employment Opportunity Commission, "The Equal Pay Act of 1963," accessed July 5, 2021, https://www.eeoc.gov/statutes/equal-pay-act-1963.

104. EEOC, "Title VII of the Civil Rights Act of 1964," accessed July 5, 2021, https://www.eeoc.gov/statutes/title-vii-civil-rights-act-1964.

105. Interview with Kessler-Harris.

106. Courtni E. Molnar, "'Has the Millennium Yet Dawned?': A History of Attitudes Toward Pregnant Workers in America," *Michigan Journal of Gender & Law* 12, no. 1 (2005), https://repository.law.umich.edu/cgi/viewcontent.cgi?referer=https://www.google.com/&httpsredir=1&article=1093&context=mjgl.

107. Roberts, *Killing the Black Body,* p. 292.

108. Becky Thompson, "Multiracial Feminism: Recasting the Chronology of Second Wave Feminism," *Feminist Studies* 28, no. 2, (Summer 2002): 336–60, https://www.jstor.org/stable/3178747.

109. bell hooks, "Feminist Theory: From Margin to Center," *Revolutionary Parenting* (South End Press, 1984) p. 133.

110. Wendy Kline, "Communicating a New Consciousness: Countercultural Print and the Home Birth Movement in the 1970s," *Bulletin of the History of Medicine* 89, no. 3, Special Issue: Communicating Reproduction (Fall 2015): 527–56, https://www.jstor.org/stable/pdf/26309056.pdf.

111. US Department of Labor, "The Pregnancy Discrimination Act of 1978," accessed July 5, 2021, https://www.eeoc.gov/statutes/pregnancy-discrimination-act-1978.

112. "The Legal Hurdles of Pregnancy Discrimination Claims," *CBS This Morning*, August 1, 2018.
113. Jack Rosenthal, "President Vetoes Child Care Plan as Irresponsible," *New York Times*, December 10, 1971, https://www.nytimes.com/1971/12/10/archives /president-vetoes-child-care-plan-as-irresponsible-he-terms-bill.html.
114. Hays, *The Cultural Contradictions of Motherhood*.
115. Susan Douglas and Meredith Michaels, *The Mommy Myth: The Idealization of Motherhood and How It Has Undermined All Women* (Free Press, paper- back edition, 2005), p. 17.
116. Debra Langan, "Mothering in the Middle and Self-Care: Just One More Thing to Do," from *Mediating Moms: Mothers in Popular Culture*, edited by Elizabeth Podnieks (McGill-Queen's University Press, 2012).
117. "Speed," YouTube, https://www.youtube.com/watch?v=Ed6g6I2-wZc.
118. Crittenden, *Price of Motherhood*, p. 2.

CHAPTER 2: PREGNANCY

1. Alessandra Biaggi, Susan Conroy, Susan Pawlby, and Carmine M. Pariante, "Identifying the Women at Risk of Antenatal Anxiety and Depression: A Systematic Review," *Journal of Affective Disorders* 191 (Feb. 2016): 62–77.
2. Patricia Waldron, "Hyperemesis Gravidarum: When Morning Sickness Is So Extreme You Can't Function," *New York Times*, May 14, 2019.
3. CDC, "Gestational Diabetes," accessed April 9, 2022, https://www.cdc.gov /diabetes/basics/gestational.html.
4. CDC, "Pregnancy Related Deaths," accessed August 15, 2021, https://www .cdc.gov/reproductivehealth/maternalinfanthealth/pregnancy-related mortality.htm.
5. Amy Roeder, "America Is Failing Its Black Mothers," *Harvard Public Health*, Winter 2019.
6. "Did Lockdowns Lower Premature Births? A New Study Adds Evidence," *New York Times*, October 15, 2020.
7. Lauren Slater, *Love Works Like This: Moving from One Kind of Life to Another* (Random House, 2002), pp. 26–27.
8. Signe K Dørheim and Malin Eberhard-Gran, "What Is the Right Level of Sick Leave among Pregnant Women?" *Women's Health, Future Medicine*, 2013, https://journals.sagepub.com/doi/pdf/10.2217/WHE.13.3.

CHAPTER 3: IDENTITY

1. Quoctrung Bui and Claire Cain Miller, "The Age That Women Have Babies: How a Gap Divides America," *New York Times*, August 4, 2018.
2. T. J. Mathews, MS, and Brady E. Hamilton, "First Births to Older Women Continue to Rise," National Center for Health Statistics Data Brief, May 2014, https://www.cdc.gov/nchs/products/databriefs/db152.htm.

3. Diana Souhami, *Mrs. Keppel and Her Daughter* (St. Martin's Griffin, eBook version, 1998), p. 42.

4. Seungmi Yang et al., "Breastfeeding During Infancy and Neurocognitive Function in Adolescence: 16-Year Follow-up of the Probit Cluster-Randomized Trial," *PLOS Medicine,* April 20, 2018, https://journals.plos.org /plosmedicine/article?id=10.1371/journal.pmed.1002554.

5. "In Sweden, It's Possible to Combine Career with Family Life. Here's Why," Sweden.se, accessed January 15, 2022, https://sweden.se/life/society/work -life-balance.

6. Karin Cato, "Breastfeeding as a Balancing Act—Pregnant Swedish Women's Voices on Breastfeeding," *International Breastfeeding Journal,* March 2020, https://internationalbreastfeedingjournal.biomedcentral.com/articles/10.1186 /s13006-020-00257-0.

7. Cato, "Breastfeeding as a Balancing Act."

8. M. Jane Heinig et al., "Overcoming Barriers to Breastfeeding in Low-Income Women," California WIC Association and the UC Davis Human Lactation Center, March 2006, https://calwic.org/storage/documents/wellness/bf _paper2.pdf.

9. Coralie L. Roll and Francine Cheater, "Expectant Parents' Views of Factors Influencing Infant Feeding Decisions in the Antenatal Period: A Systematic Review," *International Journal of Nursing Studies* 60 (Aug. 2016): 145–55, https://pubmed.ncbi.nlm.nih.gov/27297376/.

10. CDC, "Key Breastfeeding Indicators," accessed January 15, 2022, https:// www.cdc.gov/breastfeeding/data/facts.html.

11. Andrea Freeman, "First Food" Justice: Racial Disparities in Infant Feeding as Food Oppression," *Fordham Law Review,* 83 (2015): 3053, http:// fordhamlawreview.org/wp-content/uploads/assets/pdfs/Vol_83/No_6/Freeman _May.pdf.

12. Hanna Rosin, "The Case Against Breast-feeding," *Atlantic,* April 2009, https://www.theatlantic.com/magazine/archive/2009/04/the-case-against -breast-feeding/307311/.

13. Institute of Medicine (US) Committee on Nutritional Status During Pregnancy and Lactation, "Who Breastfeeds in the United States?" *Nutrition During Lactation* (National Academies Press, 1991).

14. CDC, "Key Breastfeeding Indicators."

15. Joan B. Wolf, *Is Breast Best?: Taking on the Breastfeeding Experts and the New High Stakes of Motherhood* (NYU Press, 2011).

16. Wolf, *Is Breast Best?*

17. Sharon Lerner, "The Real War on Families," In These Times, August 18, 2015.

18. Alia M. Heise and Diane Wiessinger, "Dysphoric Milk Ejection Reflex: A Case Report," *International Breastfeeding Journal,* 2011, https://www.ncbi .nlm.nih.gov/pmc/articles/PMC3126760/.

19. Interview with Kiah Bowers, July 20, 2021.

20.   Interview with Wynter Mitchell-Rohrbaugh, July 16, 2021.

21.   Interview with Kari Cobham, July 19, 2021.

22.   Interview with Angela Hatem, February 5, 2021.

23.   Rebecca Jo Plant, *Mom: The Transformation of Motherhood in Modern America* (University of Chicago Press, 2010), Kindle edition, loc 114 of 3974.

24.   Interview with "Jiah," a pseudonym, February 2, 2021.

25.   Interview with Breen Nolan Schoen, February 3, 2021.

26.   Interview with Janan Graham-Russell, February 3, 2021.

27.   Interview with Carmen C., February 2, 2021.

28.   Interview with Myra Jones-Taylor, February 23, 2021.

29.   Jennifer Glass et al., "Parenthood and Happiness: Effects of Work-Family Reconciliation Policies in 22 OECD Countries," *American Journal of Sociology* 122, no. 3 (2016).

30.   Caitlyn Collins, "Why American Moms Can't Get Enough Expert Parenting Advice," *Atlantic,* May 12, 2019, https://www.theatlantic.com/family/archive/2019/05/american-parents-obsession-expert-advice/589132/.

31.   Collins, "Why American Moms Can't Get Enough."

CHAPTER 4: WORK

1.   Robert Lowes, "FDA Approves Diclegis as First Morning Sickness Drug in 30 Years," *Medscape,* April 9, 2013, https://www.medscape.com/viewarticle/782212.

2.   Bara Fintel, Athena T. Samaras, and Edson Carias, "The Thalidomide Tragedy: Lessons for Drug Safety and Regulation," *Helix Magazine,* July 28, 2009.

3.   Nina Nuangchamnong and Jennifer Niebyl, "Doxylamine Succinate–Pyridoxine Hydrochloride (Diclegis) for the Management of Nausea and Vomiting in Pregnancy: An Overview," *International Journal of Women's Health* 6 (2014): 401–409, https://www.ncbi.nlm.nih.gov/pmc/articles/PMC3990370/.

4.   Katie Thomas, "The Unseen Survivors of Thalidomide Want to Be Heard," *New York Times,* March 23, 2020, https://www.nytimes.com/2020/03/23/health/thalidomide-survivors-usa.html.

5.   Fintel, Samaras, and Carias, "Thalidomide Tragedy."

6.   Julie Beck, "The Concept Creep of 'Emotional Labor,'" *Atlantic,* November 26, 2018, https://www.theatlantic.com/family/archive/2018/11/arlie-hochschild-housework-isnt-emotional-labor/576637/.

7.   Arlie Russell Hochschild, *The Managed Heart: Commercialization of Human Feeling* (University of California Press, 2012), p. 163, https://www.jstor.org/stable/10.1525/j.ctt1pn9bk.6.

8.   Hochschild, *The Managed Heart*, p. 170.

9.   Joan Williams, *Unbending Gender: Why Family and Work Conflict and What to Do About It* (Oxford University Press, 2000), p. 21.

10.   Jocelyn Frye, "Valuing Black Women's Work," Center for American Progress, August 7, 2018, https://www.americanprogress.org/article/valuing-black-womens-work/.

11.   Dawn Marie Dow, "Negotiating 'The Welfare Queen' and 'The Strong Black Woman': African American Middle-Class Mothers' Work and Family Perspectives," *Sociological Perspectives* 58, no. 1 (Spring 2015): 36–55, https://www.jstor.org/stable/44014691.

12.   Pronita Gupta, Tanya Goldman, Eduardo Hernandez, and Michelle Rose, "Paid Family and Medical Leave Is Critical for Low-Wage Workers and Their Families," Center for Law and Social Policy, December 19, 2018, https://www.clasp.org/publications/fact-sheet/paid-family-and-medical-leave-critical-low-wage-workers-and-their-families.

13.   Jodi Kantor, "Working Anything but 9 to 5: Scheduling Technology Leaves Low-Income Parents With Hours of Chaos," *New York Times,* August 13, 2014, https://www.nytimes.com/interactive/2014/08/13/us/starbucks-workers-scheduling-hours.html.

14.   Katherine Guyot and Richard V. Reeves, "Unpredictable Work Hours and Volatile Incomes Are Long-Term Risks for American Workers," Brookings Institution, August 18, 2020, https://www.brookings.edu/blog/up-front/2020/08/18/unpredictable-work-hours-and-volatile-incomes-are-long-term-risks-for-american-workers/.

15.   Bureau of Labor Statistics, "Employment Characteristics of Families—2020," April 21, 2021, https://www.bls.gov/news.release/pdf/famee.pdf.

16.   Ernie Tedeschi, "The Mystery of How Many Mothers Have Left Work Because of School Closings," *New York Times,* October 29, 2020, https://www.nytimes.com/2020/10/29/upshot/mothers-leaving-jobs-pandemic.html.

17.   Nikki Graf, "Most Americans Say Children Are Better Off with a Parent at Home," Pew Research Center, October 10, 2016, https://www.pewresearch.org/fact-tank/2016/10/10/most-americans-say-children-are-better-off-with-a-parent-at-home/.

18.   "Women More Than Men Adjust Their Careers for Family Life," Pew Research Center, October 1, 2015, https://www.pewresearch.org/fact-tank/2015/10/01/women-more-than-men-adjust-their-careers-for-family-life/.

19.   "2016 Land Report 100," *The Land Report: The Magazine of the American Landowner,* December 1, 2016, https://landreport.com/2016/12/2016-land-report-100/.

20.   Amanda Fortini, "O Pioneer Woman! The Creation of a Domestic Idyll," *The New Yorker,* May 9, 2011, https://www.newyorker.com/magazine/2011/05/09/o-pioneer-woman.

21.   Ree Drummond, "Roasted Greek Salad," Food Network, https://www.foodnetwork.com/recipes/ree-drummond/roasted-greek-salad-8881417.

22.   Stephen Benard and Shelley J. Correll, "Normative Discrimination and the Motherhood Penalty," *Gender and Society* 24, no. 5 (October 2010): 616–46, https://www.jstor.org/stable/25741207.

23. Shelley J. Correll, "Minimizing the Motherhood Penalty: What Works, What Doesn't and Why?" Gender & Work: Challenging Conventional Wisdom, Harvard Business School, 2013, https://www.hbs.edu/faculty /Shared%252520Documents/conferences/2013-w50-research-symposium /correll.pdf.

24. Benard and Correll, "Normative Discrimination."

25. Elizabeth Warren and Amelia Warren Tyagi, *The Two-Income Trap: Why Middle-Class Parents Are Going Broke* (Basic Books, 2016), pp. 6–7.

26. Olga Khazan, "How Welfare Reform Left Single Moms Behind," *Atlantic*, May 12, 2014, https://www.theatlantic.com/business/archive/2014/05/how -welfare-reform-left-single-moms-behind/361964/.

27. Child Care Aware of America, "The US and the High Price of Child Care: An Examination of a Broken System," 2019.

28. Ellen Bravo, "A Snow Day Cost This Woman Her Job at Whole Foods," *The Nation*, February 10, 2014.

29. US Department of Labor, "Family and Medical Leave Act (FMLA)," accessed July 6, 2021, https://www.dol.gov/general/topic/workhours/fmla.

30. Interview with Christine Hernandez, June 18, 2021.

31. US Department of Labor, "Families First Coronavirus Response Act: Questions and Answers," accessed July 7, 2021, https://www.dol.gov/agencies/whd /pandemic/ffcra-questions.

32. Interview with Dreama James, July 1, 2021.

33. Interview with Patrice Gamble, June 25, 2021.

34. Interview with "Heather," a pseudonym, June 24, 2021.

35. Interview with Alexandra Hochster, June 23, 2021.

36. Aaron De Smet, Bonnie Dowling, Marino Mugayar-Baldocchi, and Joachim Talloen, "Married to the Job No More: Craving Flexibility, Parents Are Quitting to Get It," McKinsey & Company, December 3, 2021, https://www.mckinsey .com/business-functions/people-and-organizational-performance/our-insights /married-to-the-job-no-more-craving-flexibility-parents-are-quitting-to-get-it.

CHAPTER 5: SOCIAL MEDIA

1. Irena Zakarija-Grkovic and Fiona Stewart, "Treatments for Breast Engorgement during Lactation," *Cochrane Database System Reviews,* September 2020, https://pubmed.ncbi.nlm.nih.gov/32944940/.

2. Christian Kubb and Heather M. Foran, "Online Health Information Seeking by Parents for Their Children: Systematic Review and Agenda for Further Research," *Journal of Medical Internet Research*, August 2020, https://www .ncbi.nlm.nih.gov/pmc/articles/PMC7479585/.

3. "Kindred," Parents.com, accessed April 18, 2022, https://www.parents.com /kindred/.

4. "Top 350 Mom Instagram Influencers Most Followed," blog.feedspot.com, June 28, 2021, https://blog.feedspot.com/mom_instagram_influencers/, "Top

10 Mom Influencers Across Social Media (Updated)," Neoreach, March 6, 2018, https://neoreach.com/top-mom-influencers/.

5.　Aaron E. Carroll, "What Happens When You Let Babies Feed Themselves?" *New York Times,* February 26, 2018, https://www.nytimes.com/2018/02/26 /upshot/self-feeding-babies-and-the-obesity-epidemic.html.

6.　Kathryn Jezer-Morton, "Online Momming in the 'Perfectly Imperfect' Age," *The Cut,* April 10, 2019, https://www.thecut.com/2019/04/online-moms -mommyblogs-instagram.html.

7.　"First Aid for Parents," *New York Times,* September 23, 1926, https://times machine.nytimes.com/timesmachine/1926/09/23/98393560.html?page Number=24.

8.　"Mrs. Littledale, Magazine Editor," *New York Times,* January 10, 1956, https://timesmachine.nytimes.com/timesmachine/1956/01/10/issue.html.

9.　Jessica Grose, Comment on "I'm Embarrassed by My Prenatal Depression. Here's Why I Talk About It Anyway," *New York Times,* April 30, 2019.

10.　Jessica Grose, Comment on "Parenting Was Never Meant to Be This Isolating," *New York Times,* Oct. 7, 2020.

11.　Amber Fillerup [@amberfillerup], "Life is so fun with them," Instagram, July 21, 2021, https://www.instagram.com/p/CRPebxfpnqM/?.

12.　Amber Fillerup [@amberfillerup], "The last of our AFC x @skatie_official prints drop next week! Here is a sneak peek this floral makes me so happy!" Instagram, July 7, 2021, https://www.instagram.com/p/CRB-7rqpMjI/?.

13.　Interview with Kathryn Jezer-Morton, July 13, 2021.

14.　Interview with Liz Gumbinner, July 16, 2021.

15.　Interview with Denene Millner, July 20, 2021.

16.　Interview with Millner.

17.　Interview with Gwynne Watkins, July 12, 2021.

18.　Ayelet Waldman, "Truly, Madly, Guiltily," *New York Times,* March 27, 2005, https://www.nytimes.com/2005/03/27/fashion/truly-madly-guiltily.html.

19.　Emily Matchar, "Why I Can't Stop Reading Mormon Housewife Blogs," Salon.com, January 15, 2011, https://www.salon.com/2011/01/15/feminist _obsessed_with_mormon_blogs/.

20.　Waldman, "Truly, Madly, Guiltily."

21.　Matchar, "Why I Can't Stop Reading."

22.　Kimberly Brown, "TOP MOMS: Babble.com Ranks Top 100 Most Influential Mom Bloggers," *ABC News,* December 13, 2011, https://abcnews.go.com /blogs/million-moms-challenge/2011/12/13/top-moms-babble-com-ranks -top-100-most-influential-mom-bloggers.

23.　Interview with Watkins.

24.　Interview with Millner.

25.　Kara Swisher, "Exclusive: Disney Acquires 'Sophisticated' Mommy Blog Platform Babble Media," *All Things D,* November 14, 2011, https://allthingsd .com/20111114/exclusive-disney-acquires-hipster-mommy-blog-platform -babble-media/.

26. "The Top 100 Mom Blogs of 2011: Full List," Babble.com, accessed on the
     Wayback Machine, July 18, 2021, http://web.archive.org/web/20120116084611
     /http://www.babble.com/mom/work-family/top-mom-bloggers-full-list.

27. Ingrid Lunden, "Disney Quietly Shut Down Babble, the Parenting Blog It
     Once Acquired for $40m," TechCrunch, January 7, 2019, https://techcrunch
     .com/2019/01/07/disney-babble-goes-quiet/.

28. Interview with Millner.

29. "The Influencer Marketing Industry Global Ad Spend: A $5–$10 Billion
     Market by 2020," Medikix, March 6, 2018.

30. Christine Michel Carter, "Millennial Moms: The $2.4 Trillion Social
     Media Influencer," Forbes, June 15, 2017, https://www.forbes.com/sites
     /christinecarter/2017/06/15/millennial-moms-the-2-4-trillion-social-media
     -influencer/?sh=1301e1de2261.

31. "United States Facts and Statistics," The Church of Jesus Christ of Latter-
     Day Saints, accessed July 19, 2021, https://newsroom.churchofjesuschrist.org
     /facts-and-statistics/country/united-states.

32. Jo Piazza, "A More Perfect Mother," Under the Influence, February 4,
     2021, https://podcasts.apple.com/us/podcast/a-more-perfect-mother
     /id1544171101?i=1000507685415.

33. Elder Steven E. Snow, "The Sacred Duty of Record Keeping," The Church
     of Jesus Christ of Latter-Day Saints, accessed on July 19, 2021, https://www
     .churchofjesuschrist.org/study/ensign/2019/04/the-sacred-duty-of-record
     -keeping?lang=eng.

34. Snow, "The Sacred Duty of Record Keeping."

35. "Revelations, Unpublished," The Encyclopedia of Mormonism, BYU,
     accessed on July 20, 2021, https://eom.byu.edu/index.php/Revelations,
     _Unpublished.

36. "Articles of Faith," The Church of Jesus Christ of Latter-Day Saints, accessed
     on July 20, 2021, https://www.churchofjesuschrist.org/study/manual/gospel
     -topics/articles-of-faith?lang=eng.

37. Kristine Haglund, "Blogging the Boundaries: Mormon Mommy Blogs and
     the Construction of Mormon Identity," from Out of Obscurity: Mormonism
     Since 1945, edited by Patrick Q. Mason and John G. Turner (Oxford Univer-
     sity Press, 2016), p. 241, https://oxford.universitypressscholarship.com/view
     /10.1093/acprof:oso/9780199358212.001.0001/acprof-9780199358212.

38. Interview with Caroline Kline, July 16, 2021.

39. Caroline Kline, "The Mormon Conception of Women's Nature and Role: A
     Feminist Analysis," Feminist Theology, vol. 22, no. 2 (2014): 186–202, https://
     journals.sagepub.com/doi/abs/10.1177/0966735013507856.

40. Kline, "The Mormon Conception of Women's Nature."

41. Interview with Kline.

42. Interview with Meg Conley, July 12, 2021.

43. Meg Conley, "Mommies of Instagram," Home Culture, July 7, 2021, https://
     homeculture.substack.com/p/mommies-of-instagram?s=r.

44. Interview with Farah Miller, July 15, 2021.

45. Interview with Miller.

46. Interview with Conley.

47. Nona Willis Aronowitz, "The Education of Natalie Jean," *Elle,* November 5, 2019.

48. "YouTube Money Calculator," Influencer Marketing Hub, accessed July 22, 2021, https://influencermarketinghub.com/youtube-money-calculator/.

49. Interview with Jo Piazza, July 29, 2021.

50. Meg Conley, "Mommies of Instagram," *Home Culture,* July 7, 2021, https://homeculture.substack.com/p/mommies-of-instagram?s=r.

51. Interview with Piazza.

52. Interview with Millner.

53. Sharon Pruitt-Young, "Black TikTok Creators Are on Strike to Protest a Lack of Credit for Their Work," NPR, July 1, 2021, https://www.npr.org/2021/07/01/1011899328/black-tiktok-creators-are-on-strike-to-protest-a-lack-of-credit-for-their-work.

54. @emilyjeanne333, "normalize normal," TikTok, June 29, 2021, https://www.tiktok.com/@emilyjeanne333/video/6979385350082989318.

55. "About," Studio McGee, accessed July 22, 2021, https://studio-mcgee.com/the-studio/about/.

56. Interview with Conley.

57. Interview with Conley.

58. Interview with Ilyse DiMarco, July 19, 2021.

59. Kirsten Weir, "The Lasting Impact of Neglect," *Monitor on Psychology* 45, no. 6. (June 2014), https://www.apa.org/monitor/2014/06/neglect.

60. Sarah Ockwell-Smith, "Self Settling—What Really Happens When You Teach a Baby to Self Soothe to Sleep," *So-S Parenting,* June 30, 2014, https://sarahockwell-smith.com/2014/06/30/self-settling-what-really-happens-when-you-teach-a-baby-to-self-soothe-to-sleep/.

61. Interview with Brie M. Reid, July 20, 2021.

62. Michele L. Okun, "Sleep and Postpartum Depression," https://pubmed.ncbi.nlm.nih.gov/26382160/.

CHAPTER 6: EVERYTHING FALLS APART

1. Casey McNerthney, "Coronavirus in Washington State: A Timeline of the Outbreak through March 2020," KIRO-7, April 3, 2020.

2. Eisuke Nakazawa, Hiroyasu Ino, and Akira Akabayashi, "Chronology of COVID-19 Cases on the Diamond Princess Cruise Ship and Ethical Considerations: A Report from Japan," *Disaster Medicine and Public Health Preparedness,* March 24, 2020, https://www.ncbi.nlm.nih.gov/pmc/articles/PMC7156812/.

3. CDC, "Ebola Virus Disease Cluster in the United States—Dallas County,

Texas, 2014," *Morbidity and Mortality Weekly Report,* November 14, 2014, https://www.cdc.gov/mmwr/preview/mmwrhtml/mm63e1114a5.htm.

4.   Joseph De Avila, Katie Honan, and Jimmy Vielkind, "Coronavirus Death Toll Hits 55 at One Nursing Home in Brooklyn," *Wall Street Journal,* April 17, 2020.

5.   Sharon Begley, "What Explains COVID-19's Lethality for the Elderly? Scientists Look to 'Twilight' of the Immune System," *STAT News,* March 30, 2020, https://www.statnews.com/2020/03/30/what-explains-coronavirus-lethality-for-elderly/.

6.   Claire Cain Miller, "Nearly Half of Men Say They Do Most of the Home Schooling. 3 Percent of Women Agree," *New York Times,* May 6, 2020, https://www.nytimes.com/2020/05/06/upshot/pandemic-chores-homeschooling-gender.html.

7.   Ben Casselman and Ella Koeze, "More Phone Calls, Less Shopping: How the Pandemic Changed American Lives, Down to the Minute," *New York Times,* July 22, 2021, https://www.nytimes.com/2021/07/22/business/economy/how-we-spend-our-days.html.

8.   US Bureau of Labor Statistics, "The Employment Situation—April 2020," May 8, 2020, https://www.bls.gov/news.release/archives/empsit_05082020.htm.

9.   Felipe A. Dias, Joseph Chance, and Arianna Buchanan, "The Motherhood Penalty and the Fatherhood Premium in Employment during COVID-19: Evidence from the United States," *Research in Social Stratification and Mobility,* October 2020, https://www.ncbi.nlm.nih.gov/pmc/articles/PMC7431363.

10.   Misty L. Heggeness, Jason Fields, Yazmin A. García Trejo, and Anthony Schulzetenberg, "Tracking Job Losses for Mothers of School-Age Children During a Health Crisis," US Census Bureau, March 3, 2021, https://www.census.gov/library/stories/2021/03/moms-work-and-the-pandemic.html.

11.   Interview with Leah Ruppanner, July 27, 2021.

12.   Trenton D. Mize, Gayle Kaufman, and Richard J. Petts, "Visualizing Shifts in Gendered Parenting Attitudes during COVID-19," *Socius: Sociological Research for a Dynamic World* (May 7, 2021), https://journals.sagepub.com/doi/full/10.1177/23780231211013128.

13.   Interview with Patrice Gamble, June 25, 2021.

14.   Interview with Misty Heggeness, July 26, 2021.

15.   Interview with Dreama James, July 1, 2021.

16.   Interview with Michael Madowitz, July 13, 2021.

17.   "Fact Sheet: Biden-Harris Administration Announces Child Tax Credit Awareness Day and Releases Guidance for Unprecedented American Rescue Plan Investments to Support Parents and Healthy Child Development," White House, June 11, 2021, https://www.whitehouse.gov/briefing-room/statements-releases/2021/06/11/fact-sheet-biden-harris-administration-announces-child-tax-credit-awareness-day-and-releases-guidance-for-unprecedented-american-rescue-plan-investments-to-support-parents-and-healthy-child-dev/.

18.   Care.com Editorial Staff, "This Is How Much Child Care Costs in 2021," Care.com, June 10, 2021, https://www.care.com/c/how-much-does-child-care-cost.

19. "Families with Young Children Are Burdened with Rising Debt," *Rapid-EC Study*, June 2021.

20. "A Hardship Chain Reaction," Rapid-EC, *Medium*, July 20, 2020, https://medium.com/rapid-ec-project/a-hardship-chain-reaction-3c3f3577b30.

21. American Psychological Association, *Stress in the Time of COVID-19*, vol. 1, May 2020, https://www.apa.org/news/press/releases/stress/2020/report.

22. Leah Ruppanner, Xiao Tan, Andrea Carson, and Shaun Ratcliff, "Emotional and Financial Health during COVID-19: The Role of Housework, Employment and Childcare in Australia and the United States," *Feminist Frontiers*, July 7, 2021, https://onlinelibrary.wiley.com/doi/full/10.1111/gwao.12727.

23. "Something's Gotta Give," Rapid-EC, *Medium*, September 8, 2020, https://medium.com/rapid-ec-project/somethings-gotta-give-6766c5a88d18.

24. Moira O'Neil and Nat Kendall-Taylor, "When We Talk About Mothers and Work during the Pandemic, Words Matter," Rapid-EC, *Medium*, May 7, 2021, https://medium.com/rapid-ec-project/guest-post-when-we-talk-about-mothers-and-work-during-the-pandemic-words-matter-2576a2ea967b.

25. Liana Christin Landivar, Leah Ruppanner, Lloyd Rouse, William Scarborough, and Caitlyn Collins, "Public School Operating Status During the COVID-19 Pandemic and Implications for Parental Employment," *SocArXiv*, April 8, 2021, https://osf.io/preprints/socarxiv/954yp/.

26. Jessica McCrory Calarco, Emily Meanwell, Elizabeth M. Anderson, and Amelia Knopf, "By Default: How Mothers in Different-Sex Dual-Earner Couples Account for Inequalities in Pandemic Parenting," *SocArXiv*, March 31, 2021, https://osf.io/preprints/socarxiv/hgnfs/.

27. US Small Business Administration, "Paycheck Protection Program," accessed August 1, 2021, https://www.sba.gov/funding-programs/loans/covid-19-relief-options/paycheck-protection-program.

28. Interview with "Amelia," July 30, 2021.

29. Interview with Malinda Ann Hill, July 28, 2021.

30. Interview with Theresa Peters, July 30, 2021.

31. "Overloaded: Families with Children Who Have Special Needs Are Bearing an Especially Heavy Weight, and Support Is Needed," Rapid-EC, *Medium*, December 17, 2020, https://medium.com/rapid-ec-project/overloaded-families-with-children-who-have-special-needs-are-bearing-an-especially-heavy-weight-4e613a7681bd.

32. Anya Kamenetz, "Families of Children with Special Needs Are Suing in Several States. Here's Why," NPR, July 23, 2020, https://www.npr.org/2020/07/23/893450709/families-of-children-with-special-needs-are-suing-in-several-states-heres-why.

33. Joel Wolfram, "Autism and Child Care: How a Lack of Quality Programs Hurts Families," WHYY, February 21, 2020, https://whyy.org/articles/autism-and-child-care-how-a-lack-of-quality-programs-hurts-families/.

34. Child Care Aware of America, "The US and the High Price of Child Care: An Examination of a Broken System," 2019.

35. "Overloaded: Families with Children."

36. "The US and the High Price of Child Care."

37. "The US and the High Price of Child Care."

38. Rasheed Malik, Katie Hamm, Leila Schochet, Cristina Novoa, Simon Work-man, and Steven Jessen-Howard, "America's Child Care Deserts in 2018," Center for American Progress, December 6, 2018, https://www.american progress.org/issues/early-childhood/reports/2018/12/06/461643/americas -child-care-deserts-2018/.

39. Child Care Coordinating Council of the North Country, Inc.,"Child Care Deserts in the North Country: A Region in Crisis," 2019, https://www.ccf .ny.gov/files/3515/7909/7246/drNorthCountry.pdf.

40. National Association for the Education of Young Children, "Progress and Peril: Child Care at a Crossroads," July 2021, https://www.naeyc.org/sites /default/files/globally-shared/downloads/PDFs/resources/blog/naeyc_july _2021_survey_progressperil_final.pdf.

41. Interview with Audrey, August 3, 2021.

42. Rapid-EC raw data shared with author.

43. US Chamber of Commerce Foundation, "New Study Identifies More Than $3 Billion in Annual Economic Opportunity for Pennsylvania," February 28, 2020, https://www.uschamberfoundation.org/press-release/new-study-reveals -pennsylvania-loses-billions-potential-revenue-due-inadequate.

44. Zero to Three, "The State of Child Care for Babies: The Need to Do Better for Our Youngest Children," March 10, 2021, https://www.zerotothree.org /resources/3924-the-state-of-child-care-for-babies-the-need-to-do-better-for -our-youngest-children.

45. Zero to Three, "State of Child Care."

46. Interview with Patricia Cole, August 4, 2021.

47. Zero to Three, "Parents' Just-in-Time Work Schedules Are Not Working for Babies: A Policy Brief," January 2021, https://www.zerotothree.org /resources/3874-parents-just-in-time-work-schedules-are-not-working-for -babies-a-policy-brief.

48. Dana Goldstein and Alicia Parlapiano, "The Kindergarten Exodus," *New York Times,* August 7, 2021, https://www.nytimes.com/2021/08/07/us/covid -kindergarten-enrollment.html?referringSource=articleShare.

49. Karyn Lewis, Megan Kuhfeld, Erik Ruzek, and Andrew McEachin, "Learning during COVID-19: Reading and Math Achievement in the 2020–21 School Year," NWEA.org, July 2021, https://www.nwea.org/content/uploads/2021/07 /Learning-during-COVID-19-Reading-and-math-achievement-in-the-2020 -2021-school-year.research-brief-1.pdf.

50. Emma Dorn, Bryan Hancock, Jimmy Sarakatsannis, and Ellen Viruleg, "COVID-19 and Student Learning in the United States: The Hurt Could Last a Lifetime," McKinsey & Company, June 1, 2020, https://www.mckinsey .com/industries/public-and-social-sector/our-insights/covid-19-and-student -learning-in-the-united-states-the-hurt-could-last-a-lifetime.

51. CDC, "Disparities in Deaths from COVID-19," December 10, 2020, https://www.cdc.gov/coronavirus/2019-ncov/community/health-equity/racial-ethnic-disparities/disparities-deaths.html.

52. "How Long Can the Levee Hold?" The Rapid-EC Project, *Medium,* https://medium.com/rapid-ec-project/how-long-can-the-levee-hold-2a2cd0779914.

53. Lucy Tompkins, "Here's What You Need to Know About Elijah McClain's Death," *New York Times,* February 23, 2021, https://www.nytimes.com/article/who-was-elijah-mcclain.html.

54. Interview with Tanya Ilela, August 2, 2021.

55. American Psychological Association, "Stress in America: A National Mental Health Crisis," October 2020, https://www.apa.org/news/press/releases/stress/2020/sia-mental-health-crisis.pdf.

56. American Psychological Association, "Stress in America."

57. Rapid-EC raw data shared with author.

58. "The Return of the Multi-Generational Family Household," Pew Research, March 18, 2010, https://www.pewresearch.org/social-trends/2010/03/18/the-return-of-the-multi-generational-family-household/.

59. Richard Fry, Jeffrey S. Passel, and D'Vera Cohn, "A Majority of Young Adults in the U.S. Live with Their Parents for the First Time since the Great Depression," Pew Research, September 4, 2020, https://www.pewresearch.org/fact-tank/2020/09/04/a-majority-of-young-adults-in-the-u-s-live-with-their-parents-for-the-first-time-since-the-great-depression/.

60. Tracy Hadden Loh and Evan Farrar, "The Great Real Estate Reset," Brookings Institution, December 16, 2020, https://www.brookings.edu/essay/trend-2-americas-demographics-are-transforming-but-our-housing-supply-is-not/.

61. David Brooks, "The Nuclear Family Was a Mistake," *Atlantic,* March 2020, https://www.theatlantic.com/magazine/archive/2020/03/the-nuclear-family-was-a-mistake/605536/.

62. "How Long Can the Levee Hold?" The Rapid-EC Project.

CHAPTER 7: HOW DO WE MAKE MEANINGFUL CHANGE?

1. Nicky Phillips, "The Coronavirus Is Here to Stay—Here's What That Means," *Nature,* February 16, 2021, https://www.nature.com/articles/d41586-021-00396-2.

2. Heidi Julavits, *The Folded Clock: A Diary* (Anchor, 2016).

3. Virginia Breen, "Brooklyn Protesters Slammed by NYPD SUV Vow to Keep Marching," City, June 2, 2020, https://www.thecity.nyc/2020/6/2/21278766/brooklyn-protesters-slammed-by-nypd-suv-vow-to-keep-marching.

4. Danielle Valente, "Here's How One NYC Mom Organized a Children's Protest for Equality in Brooklyn," *Time Out New York,* June 11, 2020, https://www.timeout.com/new-york-kids/news/heres-how-one-NYC-mom-organized-a-childrens-protest-for-equality-in-brooklyn-061120.

5.   Moms Moving Forward, "About Us," accessed April 18, 2022, https://moms movingforward.com/about-us.

6.   "Tigray Official Slams Damage by Troops from 'Neighbouring' Country," AFP, February 25, 2021, https://www.yahoo.com/now/tigray-official-slams -damage-troops-152009648.html.

7.   Declan Walsh, "Ethiopia's War Leads to Ethnic Cleansing in Tigray Region, U.S. Report Says," *New York Times,* February 26, 2021, https://www .nytimes.com/2021/02/26/world/middleeast/ethiopia-tigray-ethnic-cleansing .html.

8.   Simon Marks and Declan Walsh, "As Ethiopia's Civil War Rages, Bodies Float Downriver into Sudan," *New York Times,* August 3, 2021, https://www .nytimes.com/2021/08/03/world/africa/ethiopia-tigray-sudan-atrocities.html.

9.   Tigray Action Committee, "About Us," accessed April 9, 2022, https://tigray actioncommittee.com/about-us-1.

10.   Interview with Maebel Gebremedhin, July 29, 2021.

11.   Sarah Stankorb, "Where I'll Carry the Trump Years in My Body," *Medium,* January 14, 2021, https://medium.com/curious/the-lesson-well-carry-in-our -bodies-8d185cb4772c.

12.   Wyoming Community in Action, "Juneteenth is STILL ON!" June 19, 2021.

13.   Interview with Sarah Stankorb, August 4, 2021.

14.   Dr. Sheila Wijayasinghe and Anna Despina Koprantzelas, *Once Upon a Pandemic: A Pregnancy Journey* (Bella Books, 2021). https://www.onceupona pandemic.ca/our-story.

15.   UN Women, "The Shadow Pandemic: Violence against Women during COVID-19," accessed August 13, 2021, https://www.unwomen.org/en/news /in-focus/in-focus-gender-equality-in-covid-19-response/violence-against -women-during-covid-19.

16.   Interview with Sheila Wijayasinghe, July 29, 2021.

17.   Interview with Alice Kessler-Harris, July 1, 2021.

18.   Emily Cochrane and Catie Edmondson, "Manchin Pulls Support from Biden's Social Policy Bill, Imperiling Its Passage," *New York Times,* December 19, 2021, https://www.nytimes.com/2021/12/19/us/politics/manchin-build -back-better.html.

19.   First Five Years Fund, "2021 Policy Poll: Fact Sheet," January 29, 2021, https://www.ffyf.org/2021-policy-poll-fact-sheet/.

20.   US Department of Labor, "Families First Coronavirus Response Act: Employee Paid Leave Rights," accessed August 13, 2021, https://www.dol.gov /agencies/whd/pandemic/ffcra-employee-paid-leave.

21.   Gregory Svirnovskiy, "Paid Leave Is Incredibly Popular—Even with Republicans," Vox, June 7, 2021, https://www.vox.com/2021/6/7/22380427/poll-paid -leave-popular-democrats-republicans-covid-19.

22.   Svirnovskiy, "Paid Leave Is Incredibly Popular."

23.   Kaiser Family Foundation, "Paid Leave in the U.S.," December 17, 2021, https://www.kff.org/womens-health-policy/fact-sheet/paid-leave-in-u-s/.

24. Abby M. McCloskey, "Conservative Values Support Investing in Child Care as Infrastructure. Here's Why," Politico, June 17, 2021, https://www.politico.com/news/2021/06/17/conservative-values-child-care-492026.

25. Interview with Abby McCloskey, July 30, 2021.

26. Erica York and Garrett Watson, "Sen. Romney's Child Tax Reform Proposal Aims to Expand the Social Safety Net and Simplify Tax Credits," Tax Foundation, February 5, 2021, https://taxfoundation.org/child-allowance-romney-tax-proposal/.

27. Julia Cusick, "Statement: The Family Security Act Demonstrates There Is Bipartisan Urgency in Addressing Child Poverty," Center for American Progress, February 5, 2021, https://www.americanprogress.org/press/statement/2021/02/05/495513/statement-family-security-act-demonstrates-bipartisan-urgency-addressing-child-poverty/.

28. Chabeli Carrazana, "As Child Tax Credit Payments Reach Families, Moms See a Road Out of Poverty," The 19th*, July 15, 2021, https://19thnews.org/2021/07/child-tax-credit-payments-moms-road-out-of-poverty/.

29. Claire Ewing-Nelson, "All of the Jobs Lost in December Were Women's Jobs," National Women's Law Center, January 2021, https://nwlc.org/wp-content/uploads/2021/01/December-Jobs-Day.pdf.

30. Reshma Saujani, "Covid Has Decimated Women's Careers—We Need a Marshall Plan for Moms, Now," December 7, 2020, https://thehill.com/blogs/congress-blog/politics/529090-covid-has-decimated-womens-careers-we-need-a-marshall-plan-for.

31. Interview with Reshma Saujani, August 9, 2021.

32. Derek Thompson, "Workism Is Making Americans Miserable," Atlantic, February 24, 2019, https://www.theatlantic.com/ideas/archive/2019/02/religion-workism-making-americans-miserable/583441/.

33. Wesley Whistle, "Millennials and Student Loans: Rising Debts and Disparities," New America, October 29, 2019, https://www.newamerica.org/millennials/reports/emerging-millennial-wealth-gap/millennials-and-student-loans-rising-debts-and-disparities/.

34. Janet Adamy, "Millennials Slammed by Second Financial Crisis Fall Even Further Behind," Wall Street Journal, August 9, 2020, https://www.wsj.com/articles/millennials-covid-financial-crisis-fall-behind-jobless-11596811470.

35. Lynn Friss Feinberg and Laura Skufca, "Managing a Paid Job and Family Caregiving Is a Growing Reality," AARP Public Policy Institute, December 2020, https://www.aarp.org/ppi/info-2020/managing-a-paid-job-and-family-caregiving.html.

36. Nathaniel Popper, "Paternity Leave Has Long-Lasting Benefits. So Why Don't More American Men Take It?" New York Times, June 11, 2019, https://www.nytimes.com/2020/04/17/parenting/paternity-leave.html.

37. Alisha Haridasani Gupta, "In Her Words: 'Caregiving Needs Are Real,'" New York Times, August 14, 2021.

38. Gretchen Livingston, "Fewer Than Half of U.S. Kids Today Live in a 'Traditional' Family," Pew Research Center, December 22, 2014.

39. Livingston, "Fewer Than Half of U.S. Kids."

40. Katha Pollitt, "Day Care for All," *New York Times,* February 9, 2019, https://www.nytimes.com/2019/02/09/opinion/sunday/child-care-daycare-democrats-progressive.html.

CONCLUSION

1. Rozsika Parker, *Torn in Two: The Experience of Maternal Ambivalence,* new and revised edition (Virago Press, 2005), p. 7.

2. Anya Jabour, *Scarlett's Sisters: Young Women in the Old South* (University of North Carolina Press, 2007), chap. 7, https://www.jstor.org/stable/10.5149/9780807887646_jabour.11?refreqid=excelsior%3Aaec9331a297ff9c9266f9ad64d75bad4&seq=19#metadata_info_tab_contents.

Index